Reclaiming Healthy Sexual Energy

Anne Stirling Hastings, Ph.D.

Health Communications, Inc.
Deerfield Beach, Florida

Reprinted with permission from Farrar, Straus & Giroux, Inc., quote from *Thou Shalt Not Be Aware*, 1986 by Alice Miller.

Library of Congress Cataloging-in-Publication Data

Hastings, Anne Stirling
  Reclaiming healthy sexual energy/Anne Stirling Hastings.
    p. cm.
  Includes bibliographical references.
  ISBN 1-55874-117-8
  1. Sex. 2. Sex (Psychology) 3. Dependency (Psychology)
I. Title
HQ21.H3297 1991
306.7 — dc20   90-38975
                                                              CIP
©1991 Anne Stirling Hastings
ISBN 1-55874-117-8

Publisher: Health Communications, Inc.
         3201 S.W. 15th Street
         Deerfield Beach, Florida 33442-8190
Cover design by Barbara M. Bergman

This book is dedicated to
The Love of Truth
I share with Rex Holt, my life partner

AUTHOR'S NOTE

I have used the stories of many people to illustrate this book. Some are my own, some are people I have known and many are from my psychological practice. I have changed the names of all the people I present, and in most cases, any identifying information. When the stories are specific or detailed, I have received permission to use them.

ACKNOWLEDGMENTS

Carole Glickfeld is the author of the acclaimed book of short stories, *Useful Gifts*. Her "day job" is helping others with their creative projects. Carole's ability to give me penetrating criticism entirely without shame made it possible for me to hand over each chapter to her with trust that it would be well cared for. Unswerving support for my subject and my ability to create, along with suggestions that made the book lighter and more fluid, were empowering.

Rex Holt is my life partner. He is an artist with several media, including sculpture, piano, drawing and Rolfing. More important, he is a person of great courage to be married with me. I tell hard, painful truths and I demand constant examination of ourselves, our relationship and our culture. Out of this study have come deep trust and a laboratory for emotional healing and growing wisdom about healthy sexual energy.

Eileen Harrington, Libby Roderick, Gay Erickson and Joyce Marshall are models of powerful women, fully living their lives, who make room for *all* of their feelings. I value their examples.

Twilah and Tim Dugan offered me new parenting, RC style.

Vicky Lorvick, Barbara Bouchet and Jennifer Hine read manuscripts, nodded and smiled and then used what they had read in their own lives.

CONTENTS

FOREWORD

Anne Stirling Hasting's book brings out the worst in me —
my jealousy! This is a book I would have liked to have written.
Reclaiming Healthy Sexual Energy states clearly and with support
examples, the sexual issues that individuals and our culture
struggle with. Anne traces the causes of these issues from our
culture and our families and the effects of them in our lives and
relationships. She addresses what I have been dealing with in
my own recovery for 14 years. I still need all the information
and support I can find.

This is a landmark book in sexuality and sexual addiction. For
the past several years I have been doing workshops on sexuality
and intimacy. Last year, working with Marvel Harrison, we
began to call these workshops "Inside Out — Building Intimacy
From Within." When I read the concept of "inside out" and its
counterpart "outside in," I was moved by the awareness that
when an idea or concept's time has come, it will show up in
several places.

The issues of women and sexual addiction have often
stumped me but Anne clearly and gently illustrates the cultural
reinforcement for women to diffuse their sexual addiction process into love, romance and fantasy.

In 1977 another therapist and I started the first SAA program. We have seen this program grow internationally and
hope it continues. The devastation in families and our culture
from sexual addiction must be recognized and recovery made

available. Anne's book is a needed vehicle for me in my own journey and I believe it has a chance to impact the journey of anyone who reads it, sexual addict or not, for we have all learned to use sex addictively. So few of us have been supported for our sexuality. It takes courage to write on these topics and even more to share our own story in the writing. Anne's self-disclosure in modeling her writing is instructing. Thank you, Anne, for the risk and gift of your book.

Terry Kellogg

INTRODUCTION

We don't have to know precisely what is wrong sexually to begin the process of healing. It is enough to sense that something is off, something is missing, not working right or that our behaviors are somehow disturbing to ourselves and/or others. We can be sure that whatever our thoughts, feelings or behaviors, *we are not alone.*

There are untold people who pursue full-blown affairs or hasty encounters, sexual activities they believe to be "dirty" or "bizarre," as well as people who may feel only numbness during sex or distaste afterwards. Out there are people — heterosexual and homosexual — who spend countless hours daydreaming about romance or fantasizing about their next sexual encounter. And there are many who experience an "unnatural" attraction to pornography, masturbation, to partners with particular features, to sexual novelty, to voyeurism. And there are many who also feel "wronged" by partners who exhibit one or more such behaviors. *We are not alone.*

I grew up feeling something was wrong, something having to do with me and sex, but I had no language to describe what it was. Told that I was lucky to have such a wonderful family, I had to assume I was to blame for my own discomfort. In adulthood, I found out I was a sex addict long after I let go of my addictive behavior. Since then I have learned how to experience *all* of my feelings, to express them without harming myself or others, to reclaim my healthy sexual energy.

My healing comes from learning how to let my past speak, how to hear what my inner voices wish to tell me, how to become more aware. I am still learning, still growing, still reclaiming. As a psychologist specializing in sexuality, I work with sex addicts, as well as those who are numb to sex. My own healing, along with the healing of my clients, provides offerings in the chapters that follow.

Reclaiming our healthy sexuality is a journey into an exciting future, yet it requires us to travel back through our past. You may think of this book as a travel guide of sorts, pointing the way toward recovery. Like anthropologists, we will look at everything that might have influenced our sexuality. Never mind that our culture has insisted we not see, not talk, not know. We *will* see, especially parental and cultural influences that — unseen — have distorted our perceptions. We *will* talk, especially to let go of the shame. We *will* know, even if that violates the commandment, Thou Shalt Not Be Aware.

Using stories of clients, I will show that most of our sexual responses are not "inside-out" emerging of arousal but the result of conditioning from childhood and society. Forces from the past have all conspired to shame us, to make us confuse sexuality with self-worth, to make us fear sex or misuse it, to cause us to disrupt our work or other aspects of our life in pursuit of it, to escape intimacy and forego love.

To help you recover your early sexual memories, which are essential to understanding current behaviors, I have provided checklists, questionnaires and visualizations. They will also assist you to identify areas you wish to change. And because we need not change alone, I have included specific sources of outside help: books, therapies, support and counseling groups and body work. Using all the means at our disposal, we can become aware of our past, our culture, our individual "cross-wiring" of sex and our bodies. We can identify our true feelings. We can befriend our feelings. We can deepen our connection to our inner self and our spirituality.

Those of us who seek healing — from incest, from other abuse, from misguided intentions, from societal pressures, from addiction, from such effects on our loved ones — can now begin to embark on this journey of recovery. We are voyaging to the place where our sexual thoughts, feelings and behaviors emerge out of loving and where our sexual energy is healthy and health giving.

1

When Is Sex Addictive?

This chapter can help you identify what you want to change about your sexual energy. The language of addiction is useful to talk about the problems people face as they attempt to engage in one of our most basic human needs — sex, loving, coupling, beginning families and living fully in our physical, sexual selves. We will begin by looking at the characteristics of addictive sexuality so you can see which, if any, apply to you.

Sexual Energy — Healthy Or Addictive?

Sexual energy is the fuel for our natural ability to become sexually aroused and engage in sexual activity. It draws people toward each other, turning friends into lovers as sexual energy brings about bonding. Sexual bonding is seen in the outward signs of falling in love. Among them are intense looks, strong

1

interest in the other, sharing life stories, looking deeply into each other's eyes, spending large amounts of time together and sexual arousal. These are natural uses of sexual energy.

We are all born with an innocent form of this energy. Our little bodies come equipped with the ability to feel every pore and receive many kinds of information. Young people who have not yet been shamed or touched in contaminated ways feel free and joyful with the earliest forms of their sexual selves. In their innocence they can allow this energy to ebb and flow as it will. As adults we have the potential to reclaim the innocent presence of sexual feelings and joyful lovemaking.

Innocence doesn't last long. The carriers of our culture impose damaging influences on sexuality, and as young children we respond. Our sexuality changes. We learn to hide it or repress it entirely. Or else we find that it surges up and dominates our feelings even at a young age. By the time puberty arrives, the groundwork is laid for difficulty with the influence of sex hormones. No one escapes. The influences are built into our culture.

In the spectrum of adult life, a few people are able to retrieve some of the innocence they had at birth. Sometimes two people can learn together about sexual activity and sexual bonding in the privacy of their home. Others find their sex lives and coupling to be just adequate. Still others decline to participate, allowing their sexuality to remain in repression and out of touch with their lives. And finally there are those for whom sex seems like a vital need, who are caught up in the *addictive* use of it.

What Is Addiction?

Sexual energy (or drugs, TV, talking, shopping, eating, working, relationships, religion, etc.) is used *addictively* when it is repeatedly designed to avoid other feelings or awarenesses. Bob avoided feelings of impending failure and loneliness by energetically pursuing many women. If he were using sexuality in life-enhancing ways, he might choose to bring this attention into his marriage in order to develop a loving relationship with his wife. He was aware that the constant pursuit of women kept him energized and unable to feel "down" for long. He also knew that his use of sexual energy to feel alive had resulted in two failed marriages to women who responded at first to his pursuit but later felt unloved by his sexual desires.

In Chapter 10 we will look in detail at this addictive use of sexual energy to avoid feelings. For now I suggest you feed a question into your creative self and see what comes up as you read on. The question is . . .

> What is going on with my feelings right before I think about sex or plan sexual activity?

Because of the culture we live in and our unique childhoods, we all arrive at adulthood with sexual feelings that are connected with other needs. Sexual energy can fuel feelings such as the search for love, acceptance and approval. When the need seems particularly strong or the desire to escape from the pains of life seems crucial, the cross-wiring can become addictive. Bob not only avoided depressing feelings with his sexual pursuits, he repeatedly brought on strong positive feelings as he searched for a woman who would look at him lovingly.

As we will see more clearly later, we live in a society that supports addictiveness and encourages us to use most of our pleasures addictively. The expressions, "She just needs a good lay," or "I haven't had any for too long" support the belief that the absence of sex seriously impairs life. Until he violated an employee's sexual boundaries by urging her to have sex with him, my client Bob was seen as a "good old boy" who liked women. Expressions such as, "He doesn't mean any harm," "He just likes to touch the women," and "He's a red-blooded all-American boy," dismissed his behavior as just the way men are. Bob knows now that he wasn't expressing a *natural* male behavior. He was violating himself, his marriage and the women he used so he could feel energized and alive. Sexual energy had become an abused tool, no longer the joyful humanness he was born with. He is now recovering his healthy sexual energy as he examines the cross-wiring from his childhood and from our culture that has affected his use of sexuality.

Our Wires Get Crossed

Cross-wiring occurs when one of the plugs that connects sexual energy to bonding with a loved person, or to intimate sexual activity, is pulled out and plugged into some other facet of life instead.

For example, Bob learned during his therapy that he believed sexual attention meant he was loved, and because he was loved, he was safe. As a very young child he felt safe when he could get his mother's attention when needed, a requirement for children to grow well emotionally. However, he didn't get enough of this attention to be able to outgrow the need. Yearning to be looked at by his depressed mother and feeling frightened by the absence of attention, he observed how she gave attention to her lover. She looked deeply into his eyes, smiling and adoring him. *Bob created the wiring in his mind between adult, sexual love and receiving the attention he desperately needed.* The result was that as an adult whenever he felt desperate or unsafe he would look for sexual energy expressed by a woman.

Bob knew sexual attention did not *make* him safe, but at the same time he *felt* safe when he was getting it. Bad feelings disappeared. When he was feeling vulnerable his first thought was to find sexual attention. Neither of his marriages could provide sufficient sexual interest to make his inner child feel safe after the courtship phase passed. When Bob felt lonely or in fear of failure in his high-powered corporate job, he found sexual attention from flirting and affairs. The cross-wiring came to his attention abruptly when he was disciplined for sexual harassment of women he supervised. He was already in therapy for other issues, so he brought up the need for a change in his use of sexual energy. We could see that for him to rewire his sexual energy we needed to work on his experiences of insufficient attention during vulnerable years of childhood.

Do You Experience Sexual Trances?

As you learn about your sexuality, understanding the role of sexual trances can help you determine if and when you are using sexual energy addictively. Then you will be able to interrupt the addictive use and replace it with one that feels better to you. A sexual "trance" involves feelings and behaviors that resemble those experienced by addicts of drugs or alcohol. *Trances are used to mask or avoid feelings.* A true sex addict will create a trance every bit as strong and mood-altering as those created by large amounts of drugs or alcohol. The stronger the addictive compulsion, the stronger the altered state of consciousness will be.

In contrast to the trance, a natural state of sexual arousal is an expansive, pleasant feeling in the body that can be enjoyed just as it is, shared with a lover or masturbated into fuller presence. It can be easily abandoned when there is need to move on to other activities or thoughts. There is no intense need to do something with it.

Kenneth entered a trance-like state when he searched for prostitutes. The first time his wife saw it, she was frightened by the change on his face. His eyes glazed over and his coloring heightened. Addicts who spend hours masturbating or driving in search of a lover describe themselves as being in a trance or altered state of consciousness. Judgment is impaired by the self-produced "drug," to the point of interfering with return to work or home when expected and often running the risk of arrest.

A milder trance is described by addicts as a drive state they must continue. Bob found it so exciting to tell a woman to meet him at his apartment for sex in the middle of the work day that he was not aware others in the office knew what he was doing. My own experiences of a trance state occurred when I sat in class thinking about my lover, unable to concentrate on the lecture even when I willed myself to do so. I know I appeared to be in a world of my own.

Are You Addicted To Affairs?

Affairs outside a marriage or committed relationship can be one source of sexual trance. Those who have affairs as part of their addiction are addicted to the feelings of infatuation that accompany a relationship which can't settle into coupling. As with most addictive sex, the sex itself is only a small part of the experience. The trance state can occupy countless hours during the week, serving the addiction, while the actual time spent with lovers is "stolen" and brief.

Angela is a teacher who had an affair with her principal. The sex always took place quickly in surroundings that did not contribute to lovemaking because of their fear of being caught by either of their spouses or the many parents and school staff who could recognize them. This beautiful, competent young woman felt debased and shameful from her addiction to a relationship. She received nothing positive except for the distraction it provided from her difficult marriage. The affair began when she was preparing to leave her husband. She then stopped planning to get a divorce. By obsessing about her lover she couldn't pay much attention to her marriage.

The addictive use of affairs is quite different from affairs for many other reasons. People who are dissatisfied with their relationship will often find a new partner to fall in love with before leaving their partner. Other people believe they can carry on more than one sexual relationship at a time without damaging their marriage. Still others make a choice to stay in an unsatisfactory marriage and have a love relationship in addition. While these may not be healthy choices, they are not necessarily based on a compulsive need to use sexual energy to avoid awareness of their feelings.

Sexless Affairs

Sexless affairs are used as a solution to lack of satisfaction in marriages, and they are useful for the "loner" who is afraid to engage in long-term relationships. These affairs don't receive much scrutiny because they are easily rationalized. The coupled person can truthfully say they are not having sex, so believe their partner should not be jealous. The partner, however, is emotionally aware of the sexual energy present.

Loners can be in love from afar, either safely with a coupled person who won't have sex or for some other reason that prevents a true sexual relationship. I knew a man who was in love with a woman who didn't want to be sexual with him. They spent vast amounts of time together, intimately connected, and when one had a sexual relationship with someone else the other was jealous. Their relationship survived by not having sex, and yet it truly was a love affair. When my friend was preparing to form a life commitment with another woman, he realized he had always seen himself married to his sexless lover even though she refused to have sex with him. This relationship functioned to prevent him from fully experiencing the sexually bonded commitment to an available woman.

Are You Addicted To Seduction?

People who seduce for their fix are highly focused on the rituals of preparing their prospect to say yes. They often find that sex itself isn't very gratifying. Skilled flirting becomes part of the ritual and is sexually arousing in itself. As the addiction deepens toward an intense, driven need to be sexual, people in the addict's life begin objecting to the flirting, sometimes charging sexual harassment in the workplace.

As Bob was recovering from addiction to flirting and affairs, he found that even though he stopped flirting at work, the woman who had reported him for harassment continued to touch him in the ways they had both touched each other. She patted his stomach and stroked his shoulder with a smile. Each time she did so he called her attention to the violation of his boundaries and the double standard. She apologized and then did it again. She had been an accomplice to the addiction but had become distressed when it went past limits she found comfortable. I believe she was using sexual energy addictively as well. She enjoyed his sexual attention until it went past her limits, and then when it stopped she missed it.

Those who elicit seduction are usually addicted to the intense attention and hope they feel when they are vigorously pursued. Many people who are addicted to this kind of attention do not care if they have sex, often providing it because they feel an obligation.

Sheila came to see me when she was 51, ready to recover from her addiction. She spent years getting picked up and sleeping with men she cared nothing about, even though she felt unclean and filled with shame the next day. She had been searching for the love she felt she received from her father only when he had sex with her as a young girl. Her recovery began when she shifted her focus to learning how to love herself.

Other addicts of seduction engage in the flirting part of the process, get their fix and then are indignant that the partner wants to have sex. Jackie emitted sexual energy to all the men she was around, inviting their covert sexual attention. She wasn't conscious of her addictive use of sexual energy, so when men responded lustily, she was confused. When she became a mother, she stopped sending out signals. The interest from men declined proportionately, which she interpreted as a measure of her reduced attractiveness. Her first task was to become conscious of the way she had been using sexual energy. Then she could see how she had elicited reactions that she could use to avoid her feelings of unattractiveness.

Are You Addicted To Sex With Your Partner?

My addiction to the sexual trance state was always focused on a lover and on the next time I could be sexual with him. These trance feelings were so strong that the actual sexual interaction was not any more intense. I occupied many hours a day thinking about the last encounter and the one to come. When I was with my lover, it was impossible to have a spontaneous exchange because I had rehearsed it countless times.

The contrast with my current marriage is like night and day. I don't plan or anticipate sex, and it emerges spontaneously from the two of us. I experience the difference between taking my sexual energy to another person (using the other for my "needs") and allowing sexual energy to emerge out of the relationship that belongs to both of us. Instead of one of us "wanting" or "needing" the other, we co-create a passionate sexual expression. Neither of us is an object for the other.

Are You Addicted To Masturbation?

Masturbation is commonly used in addictive sexuality and can be a source of anticipatory trance states. Feeling sexual and thinking of the time and place where you can masturbate is a powerful distraction from the annoyances of real life. Many people have told me that when they experience a threat to their self-esteem, they immediately focus on going to an "adult" book store to watch videos or buy pornographic magazines to help them masturbate. As soon as the thoughts begin the trance builds, and it is impossible to worry about the danger to self-esteem. A more routine use of addictive masturbation occurs when awakening, in the shower and when preparing for sleep.

Finding Ourselves On The Continuum Of Sexual Addictiveness

The addictive use of sexual energy for each of us fits along a continuum from one, the absence of addiction, to five, the full presence of an addiction that renders life unmanageable. Most of us have used sexual energy addictively at some time. The more directed we are by the addiction and the more it interferes with a full and valuable life, the farther we are along the continuum. In addition, some behaviors will be rated farther along than others and some periods of life will be accompanied by more addictive behaviors. When I was in graduate school my sexual obsessions dropped to nothing. They returned when I was avoiding the impending end of my first marriage.

On the following page is the continuum that extends from no addiction to complete addiction. See where you fit and where you may have fit at other times in your life. What you learn here will be helpful when you are doing the exercises designed to heal your use of sexual energy.

CONTINUUM OF SEXUAL ADDICTIVENESS

1. The complete lack of addictiveness. Our culture makes the possibility extremely slim. Sexual activity emerges out of your relationship as an expansion of intimacy that is already occurring. Masturbation is self-loving, focused on knowing yourself.

2. Activities are completely acceptable by our society. Basic quality of life is not disrupted. Thoughts and activities are used to distract you from some general feeling of absence or emptiness in life, often called boredom. Sex or romance seems appealing to meet needs not being met in other ways. Masturbation is often "something to do." A person at this level is not addicted to sexual energy, but is using it addictively.

3. Sex seems to be the most important facet of life. You use a large percentage of your time to think about and plan for sexual encounters or masturbation. You know what a sexual trance state is like and enjoy it because it brings pleasure when life holds little elsewhere. You take occasional risks, such as having an affair or buying a prostitute, and then feel remorse and fear when you return to clear thinking. You find it distressing, even frightening, if your partner wants sex less than you do. The purpose of masturbation is to administer the sex drug. The addiction is underway.

4. You feel driven and must be sexual, with feelings of urgency and pressure. You are consumed by the need to do it again and again, and the sexual trance state becomes a greater part of your life. Thoughts and intense sexual feeling focus on the search, the person or the place that will make everything all right. For periods of time life is unmanageable, but you have sufficient ability to concentrate on non-sexual things to be able to pull it back together once again. A person at this level is truly addicted.

5. Sexual activities have resulted in severe consequences, such as loss of family, loss of job or arrest. Great amounts of time are lost to the pursuit of sexual activity. Money is spent with no regard for the consequences. Life is totally unmanageable.

Addictive Behaviors: Obsessions And Compulsions

It is convenient to divide addictive behaviors into two categories. One is the thoughts about sexual activities, the *obsessions*. The other is the activities themselves, the *compulsions*. Their obsessive and compulsive nature are what identify the thoughts and activities as addictive. How hard are they to resist?

Healthy sex emerges out of the moment or is an expression of a relationship. Addictions come from an intense "need."

What Are Your Obsessions?

Obsessing about sex can occur at the number two level of the addictiveness continuum, where mild thoughts are designed to improve life. At this level the interference with life is mild. As obsessing moves to level three, where sex seems like the most important facet of life, it more seriously interferes. Obsession can reach levels four to five, seriously impairing life.

Kitty came to therapy because her life felt totally empty and she considered ending it because she didn't feel liked by anyone. She was addicted to a number of things, including food, sleep, alcohol, romance novels and television. When we began therapy, she spent almost all her waking hours working or in bed. She perpetuated a sexual trance by reading romance novels and imagining herself in the story line. As she dealt with her addictions, she became more engaged in life, finding activities that had meaning to her.

Even if no sexual acts are involved, thoughts can make up the entire addiction. Fantasy can bring on intense sexual arousal for some people as easily as sexual touch does for others. Yearning and searching are part of the desire to find whatever will *provide safety from bad feelings*. Romance novels can be an adjunct for the addict who obsesses. Some men spend most of their sex lives looking at "sexy" women and imagining what it would be like to have sex with them.

If you find yourself frequently lost in sexual thought, the contents of the fantasies are a valuable source of information. *Note the kinds of feelings that accompany them.* It might be searching and yearning, or it could also be angry feelings. If sexual energy has become cross-wired with the expression of anger, or if you were emotionally deprived and are angry about it, these feelings can find expression in fantasy about sex. As you study cross-wiring in Chapter 12, fantasies can provide useful information to uncover the source.

Sexual energy expresses distress from childhood, and each childhood is unique. One sex addict may be primarily aroused by videos of people having sex, while another must have human contact and another is gratified only by seduction. Cross-wiring accounts for the *form* addiction takes, but its presence does not necessarily mean that a person will use sexual energy addictively.

Cross-wiring that is not addictive may be expressed in the requirement that a partner have certain characteristics in order to be sexually arousing. The requirement is not addictive because it doesn't avoid feelings. One example is our culture's valuing of thinness. Many people believe they can only be sexually attracted to a thin person. While this severely limits the choice of sex partners, it doesn't necessitate obsessive or compulsive sexual relating. The exercises in this book designed to unwire cross-wiring can be helpful if you use sexual energy addictively. They can also be useful if you don't like the non-addictive ways your sexual energy has been cross-wired.

In my own use of sexual energy, my obsessions were so subtle that it was hard to see they were addictive. I often brought to mind a picture of a man with his arms around me holding me safely. If I was in a relationship, I would imagine the man I was with at the time. But during the years I wasn't with anyone, I still did it.

I became conscious of this one day when I was paying my check at a restaurant. The cashier told me the amount I owed and I nodded. After a moment he told me again, and again I nodded, waiting for him to hand me my credit card and slip to sign. I wondered why he was telling me and looking expectant. We hadn't had any disagreement about the amount. Then it dawned on me that I had not given him my credit card, and with unspoken embarrassment I handed it over.

As I turned to walk out I found myself flooded with sexual energy and the feel of loving, warm arms around me. The feelings of shame brought on by making a mistake immediately melted into the past as the obsessive thought succeeded in taking it away. I was startled into awareness of what I had been doing my whole life. Now I could choose to stop the arms from taking away the shame so I could have a look at it. Instead of removing the feeling, I began to examine situations that brought up shame and to change the causes of obsession. I became willing to feel shame to learn about it.

I began to see all the places where this obsessive thought replaced my real feelings. The arms appeared every time I walked past the office of a very fat woman where I worked. They protected me from my feelings of what it would be like to be unattractive to men and live alone the rest of my life. This wasn't what was happening for that woman, but my imagination thought so. Arms appeared when I was bored, when I was hungry and especially when I was lonely.

I discovered this long after I had abandoned the obsessive sexual thoughts accompanying infatuation. As I healed from obvious addiction, more subtle maneuvers became apparent.

When my first marriage was ending I had a brief sexual encounter with a man I met at a workshop. We went our separate ways but communicated occasionally. I developed an obsession for this man, thinking about him all the time. Thoughts intruded into my therapy sessions and reduced my effectiveness in my work. I had a hard time getting to sleep and I woke early. I lost weight because I slept poorly. When I was with friends I wasn't really there with them. I was incapable of feeling lonely because I was filled with yearning and fantasy. I actually liked time alone so I didn't have to put an expression on my face to hide what was happening inside.

I didn't look like a sex addict. I was actually having very little sex. And yet my misuse of sexual energy was interfering with enjoying my life. It was also interfering with knowing that the time was coming to move on from my marriage.

I had believed during 17 years of marriage that sex outside the marriage would automatically end it, and now I had taken that step. By becoming addictively compulsive over this man, I successfully avoided thinking about the state of my marriage for another six months. When I broke the news to my husband at last, the addictive thinking disappeared. *There was no more need for distraction because I had addressed the reality.*

I saw this man years later at another convention and was amazed to see that he was just an ordinary person. In my fantasies I never saw him at all. I felt sexual sensations and sexual energy dripping from each of us to the other, but he was not distinct. The addiction had nothing to do with him. He was only my object.

Making Friends With Your Obsessions

What are the sexual thoughts and fantasies that wander through your mind? Include both positive and negative ones. At this point it is not necessary to decide whether they are obsessions. Take some time now to write out your experiences as I have. Write as if you are writing a letter to someone you trust, telling them the story of your sexual thoughts. Including details will make it more informative for you.

As I wrote I was surprised to find new connections. My untold memories felt complete, but an untold memory lies in our brains — formless and all the same color until it takes shape during the telling. Take as much time as you need. This is an important step. You are identifying just what is troublesome so you can fully feel what it is that you want to change. As you write, *breathe*, and welcome the feelings that arrive along with the words.

Do You Have Compulsions?

Addictions can be categorized into obsessions (thoughts) and compulsions (actions) that are dominated by sexual energy. Addictive compulsions can be described as "choosing" to have sexual activity at times, in places or with people you would not choose if thinking clearly.

Compulsions take many forms. Some common ones are . . .

- Pursuing sex partners relentlessly until they agree to sex
- Frequently seducing or being seduced by strangers
- Going to video booths in "adult" book stores to watch videos and masturbate
- Masturbating while driving and searching for the perfect partner who must be out there somewhere
- Leaving work at undesirable times to masturbate or have sex with a partner
- Buying prostitutes
- Agreeing to sex to meet the other's "need"
- Feeling unable to turn down sex

- Finding oneself in dangerous situations "accidentally" while pursuing sexual attention
- Becoming a regular at "strip joints"

If you find yourself unwilling to turn down your favored activities, even in the face of disrupting your life, you can assume you are responding compulsively.

Kenneth is a dynamic loving person who was surrounded by friends and family even in the depths of his addiction. His life looked successful because he was educated, wore expensive clothes and people loved him. His marriage was seen as a model by friends. Yet he led a double life.

Kenneth's sex addiction began when he was about 16 and discovered pornographic magazines in the garbage dump. He would go out at night searching through the trash and bring them home. A person who is not addicted to sexual energy would find this behavior strange. It only made sense as I learned about the feelings that accompanied the search. The moment he decided to go to the dump, the sexual arousal was underway, fueling the need to search that characterized all his sexual activities. This need to search was so intense that he risked being seen in a town where he was known as a model young person.

The cross-wiring that motivated his addiction was searching for love from a woman who would not be available to him. In the beginning it was women in pictures. It moved on to searching for prostitutes at times when they would not be on the street and finally on to "love" relationships with women who could not give themselves to him for various reasons. When a woman did respond sexually to him, even if he paid for it, he felt as if he were receiving the greatest loving possible. When he completed the exchange and went home, however, he was fully aware that he had not been loved at all. He could see the cross-wiring — until addiction took over again, putting him in another sexual trance.

During therapy Kenneth became aware of how he invited drug-like trances and how he exacerbated them. As he retold his activities he came to see they began when he felt he was not a valued person or felt hurt from situations where he didn't know the rules and was expected to follow them. Either of these situations was intolerable. So he would take his sexual energy "drug" by buying a magazine or searching for a woman walking down the street about whom he could fantasize.

Over time the effect of the drug was less and less, much as the effect of alcohol and other drugs diminish with constant use. It takes more to have the same results. So he would create more by masturbating while going to places that frustrated his search for the right woman who would want his penis/him and see him as the "big boy" he always wanted to be for his mother. He damaged his penis by tying it up to keep it erect when he tired of rubbing it. He had to work hard to keep his drug going and had learned many maneuvers to intensify the trance that was made up of both sexual energy and desperate searching. As with most sex addicts, the rituals — such as preparing to go to the dump and planning to drive on a certain street looking for a certain kind of woman — were just as important as the sexual stimulation itself.

Making Friends With Your Compulsions

This exercise can help bring your secrets to awareness and begin the process of reducing your feelings of shame about them. Take some time now to write about your sexual and romantic *activities*. It isn't necessary to decide whether they are compulsions. Include both positive and negative ones, giving yourself time to let them come to mind. Then let your mind wander over those times when you felt gripped by a force outside yourself and had to give in. Write as if to a trusted friend you know will accept you as you are, ready to unburden yourself of this secret.

When Are You Being Addictive?

My clients often ask me how they can tell if their thoughts and activities are addictive as they move along in the process of recovery and no longer find themselves pulled to the clearly addictive use of sexual energy. The answer that makes intuitive sense to me is to check whether thoughts or actions are narrowing down and constricting your experience of life or are opening up and enhancing it. *Addiction searches for the most immediate pleasure and prevention of pain.* This is quite different from a life that is expansive — open to the pain of grief, the despair of healing from loneliness and the enriching joy of living life fully.

I developed a test while healing from addictive maneuvers. When I have a strong interest in doing something or thinking about an idea I am having, I sometimes find I am temporarily excluding other parts of my life. Because I know this can be essential to creative and healing processes, I don't automatically assume that I am being addictive. I check it out by using the following visualization. This lets me know if my intense focus is expanding me or if it is avoiding something.

Visualization: Narrowing Down (addictive) Or Opening Up (life-enriching)

Close your eyes, breathe deeply and relax all your muscles, beginning in your toes and working up to your scalp. (If you do not have your own methods of relaxation, see Appendix II for instructions.) When you are ready, imagine yourself in a familiar situation where you are questioning whether the action you are about to take is addictive or expansive. Allow yourself to see the room. Who else is present? Hear the sounds, smell the smells and see the colors.

What are you feeling? When you are fully in the scene, then do two things. You can do them in any order or switch back and forth between them.

1. Imagine that you are slowly opening your arms, moving them gently but powerfully out to the side of your body. First imagine you are encompassing the entire world. How does it feel? Then turn your hands out as you imagine you are giving to the entire world. How does this feel? Let your arms decide where they want to move to give you the fullest feeling of opening. Will the action you want to take fit with this feeling?

2. Imagine that your hands are in front of your face, creating a limited space for you to see through. On the other side is the action you are considering. Study it. How does it feel? Will the action you want to take fit with the limited feeling?

The above visualization can provide information as you work on differentiating which of your decisions are addictive and which are life-enriching. I know that when I sat in class, unable to hear the teacher because I was in sexual fantasy, I was in an addictive place. My education was diminished by the fantasy. Sexual energy trance limits life to the focus of the trance. Sexual energy and the object of it are all that can be seen.

When I discovered that the brief thought of a man's arms around me was designed to remove feelings of shame, it was a more difficult call. Why not bring on this warm feeling occasionally? It didn't seem to interfere with my life. But it did interfere. It kept me from knowing about my feelings of shame so I couldn't examine the causes for them and let them go.

This visualization allows me to tell when I am bringing myself pleasure addictively or openly and whether my pain is addictive or useful. Perhaps you can create your own visualization test. It might be more effective than using one I created for myself.

We Can Recover Our Healthy Sexual Energy

It is possible for us to raise our consciousness about the effects of our culture. It is possible for us to define sexuality so we no longer need respond to the countless pressures to be sexual in harmful ways. It is possible to see clearly when a person or an advertisement attempts to engage us by using our sexual energy and to chuckle as we don't respond. It is also possible to learn about childhood conditioning that interfered with our delighted use of sexual energy and to let go of these influences. Those of us who are struggling with sexual addictiveness can practice the 12 Steps of Alcoholics Anonymous, which have been time-tested and work well for sexual issues.

We can recover our innocent, childlike experience of our bodies and our sexuality.

Do You Relate With Sex Addicts?

If you don't identify with sex addiction but find that what society puts forth doesn't feel right to you, this book is for you too. The methods presented here can help you learn about your real sexual nature so you can be true to it. Many people find themselves disagreeing with partners, movies and friends, but have no mirrors to reflect the accuracy of their perceptions. With the help of this book you can create your own mirror and find other people who can reflect you.

Jenny's husband brought her to me because he was distressed over her lack of interest in sex. He learned that I specialize in innocent sexual energy and hoped it meant I would encourage her to be open and free with her sexuality in ways that would please him. Instead, I said her feelings of not wanting to join him in his "free" sexual pursuits were self-respecting. Jeff wanted to have sex at least every day and was encouraging her to have sex with him and another woman. He also wanted her to join him in a swinger's club. These behaviors did not necessarily indicate that he was a sex addict (although they do indicate severe cross-wiring), but the compulsiveness with which he addressed them was addictive. In addition, his attention to sex increased dramatically when he was failing in his work. The sex drug was used to avoid feelings of failure.

Jeff's distress is evident in the escalating addiction and his attempts to control her into taking care of his "needs." His sexuality has long since left the place where it felt fun and erotic to have frequent sex with a woman he loved.

He is terrified of losing his wife because his sexual gratification requires a willing partner and because he is bonded to her and their child. Yet he can't control his desire to feed his sexual addiction. As Jenny changes as a result of her work with me, he will reach a crisis point because she won't stay with him if he does not begin recovery. It is likely that one of two things will happen. He may go further into his addiction to avoid the pain of the ending marriage, or he could feel that he has hit bottom and decide it is time to pull himself out from under the addiction.

Jenny was relieved at the end of our first session. However, it was many more weeks before she was able to see that her husband's wishes were not healthy for her and that her own understanding of the role of sex in marriage was far more accurate. Because she didn't discuss sex with anyone but him (typical in our sexually silent culture) she had no other mirrors for her suspicions that his activities were not healthy. She had only his constant pressure to "do what she said she would" when they got married — to have sex every day. As a sex addict he was concerned about "protecting his supply" of his drug — his wife.

If you are feeling you "should" be doing things you aren't comfortable with, please examine them and possibly speak to a therapist if you need a mirror. It is important to differentiate between beliefs that are in your own best interest and a fear of sex that may be holding you back from enjoying your sexual self. After the sexual revolution our culture condoned impersonal sex outside relationships. It has always condoned impersonal sex within marriage. If you are being sexual because you are married, or someone is subtly putting you down because you aren't responding to sexual overtures, then you are violating yourself. You can say no.

As we move on now to explore the backdrop for addiction, we'll begin by looking at the influences of childhood as family and other adults passed cultural distortions onto us. We'll look at the culture we live in and how it has prepared us to use sexual energy in uncomfortable ways. Then we'll take a look at adult experiences that also influenced our views of sex, before we go on to the tasks of healing.

2

The Power Of Childhood Shaming And Other Early Influences

Living in a society that doesn't talk about sex, doesn't provide good role models and has little solid information about healthy sexuality, has made it impossible for any of us to have received good parenting or to do well with our own children. The path to retrieve understanding is blocked until we can see our cross-wired uses of sexual energy and the abuses that brought them about.

The rules of our culture and the formative influences on our parents and other adults have been passed on to us as children. This chapter will look at the main ways this occurs, which fall into the following categories:

- The general shaming of sexuality that pervades our lives
- Incest experiences
- Non-family child sexual abuse
- Triangulated or other kinds of relationships with parents
- Emotional incest.

Chapter three will address the effect our culture has on sexuality.

Sexual Shaming

Shaming As A Discipline Technique

Shame is a disciplinary tool used by many parents who believe they must control sexuality in their children. Such discipline is useless and brings instead repression, rebellion and cross-wiring of sexual energy. Parents feel they must shame children to train them to control sexual impulses. This attitude has resulted in passing along erroneous information about the nature of sexual energy. Because each of us has been shamed we believe the only method of controlling sexual expression is shame, and this belief has become institutionalized in our culture. People find it difficult to recognize that the route to responsible, loving sexual activity involves *reducing* feelings of shame and *not shaming* sexual expression.

The overlay of shame on sexuality prevents us from knowing what our sexual energy could be. The use of shame is based on a belief that sexual energy is wild and unmanageable and would get out of control if external restraints were not in place. Everyone would be masturbating in public and having sex indiscriminately with no regard for the feelings of others or for loving relationships. Ironically, these very things happen *because there is too much shame.*

Toxic Shame Is Destructive

Shame is a destructive motivator and serves to inhibit the natural, "inside-out" motivators. I was monogamous during my first marriage because I was terrified of losing my husband if I had sex outside of marriage and I would have felt deeply shameful. I had no information or intuition that there were any other reasons for monogamy. After my divorce, when I could give myself permission to be sexual whenever I felt like it, I had the opportunity to remove feelings of shame from my decisions and examine the real reasons for choices. During this time I learned from the inside out that it was not right for me to have sex with a man who was married, even if he were not living with his wife. I also discovered in my second marriage the inside-out reasons for monogamy — reasons that had nothing to do with cultural rules, shame or teaching by our families.

When my son reached the age where he delighted in his penis and clearly had sexual feelings, I felt blessed to be able to interact with him differently than my parents had with me. His father and I were intrigued with his desire to run down the sidewalk with no clothes on, wagging his penis at anyone who would look. However, when my mother came to visit my comfort level dropped and I knew I was sending out unspoken messages to him not to be so open when she was around. He received the messages that he should hide his sexuality and that his mother at times felt shame about what he was doing. In addition, I learned well the rule that I couldn't talk openly about sexual things, so I was unable to comfortably talk with him. I could interact without shame so he didn't cut off his delight in his sexuality, but I was unable to go another step and talk with him about it freely.

When he reached puberty, I could see the results of both my minimal feelings of shame about sexuality and my inability to comfortably talk about it. He shyly came to us to say that he was getting pubic hair and he wanted to have a "puberty party." We took him out to dinner to celebrate his changing status — not having any other rituals available for this event! However, it was some years before I realized the transition probably wasn't pubic hair but having his first ejaculation. He intuitively knew his parents wouldn't be comfortable celebrating such an event because his father had not discussed it with him and he had perceived my discomfort when I explained it to him a year before. In addition, the subject of sex had been conspicuously absent at home after about age four.

Even now I believe if a young man asked me to help him celebrate his first ejaculation I might have some emotional work to do before being able to smile delightedly and welcome him into young adulthood. When my son told me when he had sex for the first time, I had all kinds of emotional reactions. I was torn between sharing in his experience, my feelings that he was growing up *very* fast (I still clearly remember when he was born) and the awareness that he was talking about the forbidden subject with his *mother!* And this was with substantial preparation. He had already told me he and his girlfriend were talking about it. I had counseled him on contraception and I had seen evidence of their sexual attachment for some time.

Direct Shaming

Shaming is communicated in many direct ways, too. One of my clients was severely scolded for touching his genitals and his hands were tied to the headboard to prevent masturbation when he was growing up. Many clients have talked about shaming of their genitals when they were children.

Sexuality is often associated with evil. The majority of us grow up knowing we are sexual beings, while receiving the instruction that being sexual is bad. Such dual information makes it impossible for us to feel comfortable in our bodies and self-loving. We feel like aliens who are cursed with these physical feelings in a world that seems to be devoid of them.

Feelings Of Shame Come From Sexual Violation

The other extreme from shaming and secrecy is where a family's sexual energy is out in the open, spilling onto children. Some examples are flirting with a child, patting or stroking body parts in a manner reserved for lovers and using endearing names in ways that are associated with coupling (Doll, Babe or Lover, for example).

Many years ago I was very uncomfortable with the way a friend held his three-year-old daughter on his lap, but at the time I didn't understand the nature of sexual energy. He held and stroked her in ways I would expect him to touch his wife. His wife didn't act as if anything were wrong, so I attributed my discomfort to my own "issues." On the contrary, such children feel violated by sexual energy and confused because no one comes to their rescue. The young mind makes assumptions that the self isn't worthy of protection and must be defective in some way. This child's mother and I were so indoctrinated that we were unable to see that she needed our protection.

A third kind of family ascribes to the suppression of sexuality in children, but at the same time expresses sexual energy. An example is the mother who wishes to eliminate evidence of sexuality in her children. Mothers of several of my clients wore clothes that hid their bodies and insisted their children do the same. I have heard stories from men clients whose mothers or other relatives shamed them with frowns or agitated body messages for evidence of masturbation or erections. While the parent is trying to eliminate sexual energy, the preoccupation with it is perceived by the child. This is particularly confusing to children, who must believe their perceptions are invalid. It is more difficult for children to know that their caretakers are violating them.

Sexual Shaming Brings Cross-Wiring

Sexual shaming leads to cross-wiring of sexual energy. One culturally supported example is the experience of forbidden sex as more exciting and arousing than sex with a long-term partner. It is not common knowledge that this is due to massive associations of sexual energy with the shamed and forbidden. We weren't allowed to talk about sex, to ask questions or to have our aroused feelings while we were with family members.

Even in the least abusive families, children touching their genitals in curiosity or self-arousal is not accepted. Masturbation is universally believed to be an inferior or damaging use of sexual energy, yet it is also a nearly universal activity. *The message that we are not to be sexual results in sexual arousal becoming associated with the forbidden.*

Some people respond with heightened, intense arousal when engaged in forbidden sexual activities. Others are only comfortable being sexual when they are safe in their bedrooms where no one can see.

Cross-wiring can also be seen in the woman who puts out sexual energy with body posture and facial expressions, triggering the conditioned responses of men around her. A woman I will call Lee grew up with a mother who shamed her by telling her she was a slut. We can guess that as a young person she was trying to tell her story of childhood sexual abuse with her body and manner. She received only judgment because her mother, of course, didn't know how to interpret the behaviors. As an adult she continues to tell her story in unconscious ways. Men respond to her with their own cross-wired, acculturated behaviors, which she experiences as confirmation of her cross-wired beliefs that men are only interested in sex. Until she can unravel her past and discharge her feelings about her sexual abuse, she will continue to express her distress in ways she cannot see.

The men's reactions will seem initiated by them, and she will feel re-abused by their behavior.

Shame-Based Sexual Repression

Even well-repressed sexuality makes its appearance somehow. Lee exhibited sexual energy in ways she wasn't aware of, as her sexual energy demanded some kind of manifestation. I have looked at many pictures of clients who felt asexual during earlier years, yet their pictures exhibited flirtatiousness. The movie *Sex, Lies and Videotape* portrayed this dynamic. In the beginning of the film Anne is not interested in having sex with her husband (who we later find out is having an affair with Anne's sister), and yet we see sexuality in her posture, facial expressions and tone of voice. As the movie goes on she brings her sexuality out from under repression and experiences it directly, and at the same time she no longer sends out sexual signals. Her sexual energy has become hers, *to use as she chooses*, no longer demanding expression in covert ways.

As women and men express their sexual energy in indirect ways and pick up each other's indirect sexual expression, it results in tremendous confusion about what is going on. Each sex feels victimized by the other — lied to, seduced and ever suspicious of each other.

Lee put out sexual energy during a meeting with peers by bringing attention to her breasts with her hands and making a sexually suggestive remark. Several men responded with further sexual comments. Later, when a friend brought it to her attention, Lee felt she had done nothing to trigger these responses and attributed the men's statements to their own sexual training. Her repression made it difficult for her to see that she was expressing herself sexually in ways that invited them to do the same. If she is able to examine her childhood sexual abuse (of which she is consciously aware) and relinquish the effects on her current expression of her sexuality, she will find men will rarely initiate sexual exchanges that feel violating and objectifying.

Sexual Shaming Leads To General Feelings Of Shame

The shaming of our sexuality does not attach itself only to our sexual energy. When we feel shame for one aspect of ourselves, it creates a general sense of badness that shows up in many ways.

People who are recovering from sexual shame experience intense shame when they begin to open doors to repressed feelings. They often feel like bad people and are sometimes suicidal. However, as they express shame and release it from the body and psyche, an amazing thing happens. Shame lifts also from those other areas to which it had generalized.

Carla, a client of mine, experienced deep despair as she allowed repressed memories into awareness. For many weeks she wondered if she should go into the hospital. She felt deep loneliness as memories of incest flooded back. As the shame intensified on its way out of her body, it seemed to dominate her feelings about everything she did from talking with grocery clerks to her employment. She was sure she was unable to do anything right or to maintain relationships. However, once enough shame had flowed out, she found her shame level dropping in all areas. She fell in love with herself and began to enjoy being alone. She was able to comfortably set boundaries in her work, to feel less competitive and to let go of goals and behaviors that were designed to achieve status. Instead, she became freer to do what was intuitively right for her.

Incest — Sexual Abuse By Family Members

The Complexity Of Incest

Researchers and professionals are finding that incest is far more common than was suspected only a couple of decades ago, when it was seen as a rare occurrence and a sign of severe perversion. During two years as a social worker with a county welfare department, I encountered only one recognized case of family incest. We were not aware when incest was present. We had no training to recognize signs and the victims did not talk about it. Each child victim thought she or he was the only one. Each grew into adulthood with that secret. The resulting shame and cross-wired sexuality turned victims into people who were too threatened to reveal themselves. Ironically, many were friends with other victims but were unable to reveal the secret, perpetuating the aloneness. We can now assume that a large proportion of our population have been sexually abused.

In the past decade things changed rapidly. Organizations were created to help all members of the incest-affected family and a great deal of information has emerged about how to help people. Most potent is that it has become *easier to talk about*. Others don't react with alarm as they might have 20 years ago. Many professionals have received training, and most of us have worked with those who are dealing with issues arising from incest.

Incest takes more than one form. The most overt is direct sexual contact of a child by an adult family member. The powerful adult uses the powerlessness and dependence of the child — and often the child's love for the parent — to engage in behavior that is damaging to the child's developing sexuality, emotional development and sense of self-worth.

While the most commonly discussed form of incest is that occurring between a father or father-figure and a daughter, it also occurs between fathers and sons, mothers and sons, and mothers and daughters. Sibling incest is also commonly reported for children of both sexes.

Some parents are loving and gentle when sexual with a child, with no force or coercion. Young children are sexually stimulated by the sexual activity and many enjoy it. Memory of the pleasure produces guilt and shame in adults because they believe they should have stopped it and were responsible for the abuse. An important task of healing is to know that as children we had no responsibility and no power.

Being unable to say "no" to this intrusion is terrifying to a young child. The young mind believes that saying "no" to a powerful parent will mean certain annihilation.

Another variety of incest occurs when the parent and child become lovers and the child accepts the role of surrogate spouse. The child experiences being in love with the parent and sometimes wishes to be a life partner. This kind of incest is particularly difficult to heal from because of the complexity of interwoven jealousy and desire. Those who have come to me for therapy did so to heal from the loss of a loved person after the incest was over. The abandonment is devastating because it involves so much loss: the loss of a loving parent, a sexually bonded partner and the most powerful person in the victim's life.

There seems to be a common belief that all children experience incest only negatively. It is not that simple. Each incest relationship is fraught with all the complexities of adult sexual relationships, including jealousy, possessiveness, hate, love, yearning for love and intense sexual bonding, even when the child feels traumatized by the sexual relating and wishes it to stop. (There is a direct parallel to women in abusive marriages.) Additional complications are the powerlessness and dependence of the child, isolation from the other parent brought about by the secrecy, acceptance of guilt by the child and a host of other variables. In *My Father's House*, Sylvia Fraser portrays her history of incest with both the loved feelings she received and the belief that she would no longer be loved if she refused to cooperate. At the same time she hated and feared her father.

Two factors, feeling loved by the parent and feeling powerful, are vitally important in understanding the guilt and shame that come from sexual abuse. Imagine children who are inadequately loved (which is true for most of us) receiving the intense attention of the most powerful person in their lives. Would they turn it down because it also felt violating and shameful? This attention allows the child to feel the power of being valued by the guarantor of life. To feel such power and "love" during the most vulnerable time of life is not something that can be turned down. Refusing to participate or telling someone are luxuries the child cannot afford. The price the child then pays is guilt — feeling responsible for having caused the incest.

The myriad feelings associated with sexual abuse will create cross-wiring of sexual energy with other things such as power, love, attention, competition, shame, hiding, etc. The cross-wired sexual energy can manifest as heightened sexual arousal and drive, as romantic bonding or as inhibited sexual expression.

Anna's Story

When Anna began her therapy with me for chronic depression, she had no idea she had been sexually abused. Her story demonstrates how it is possible for different kinds of cross-wiring to emerge out of childhood incest. She had been depressed and withdrawn from before age six. We worked successfully on the depression in many ways. As it lifted, Anna was able to allow into consciousness the information that she had been sexually triangulated into her parents' marriage as a young child. Working with early sexual memories and imagery, we slowly identified what had happened so she could experience her feelings about it and let go of the patterns that had been formed. Her mother was able to offer additional information that helped Anna re-create a picture. Anna's father had died so she was unable to confront him.

We reconstructed that Anna's father was sexual with her as a young child. He did not understand the boundaries of sexual activity necessary for growing children who are not able to set them. He was not able to use his intuitive capacity to understand the needs of others. He held the common view that children don't remember their early years and won't be affected by what happens to them.

When Anna was a baby he rubbed her anus with his finger, exploring how it goes through changes. The anus tightens up when touched, but with the development of sexual arousal, it opens and allows penetration. Anna's therapy work brought to consciousness the information that she found the touch uncomfortable until her sexual arousal permitted responsiveness to the touch. With each succeeding encounter, her body became aroused quickly so she would not feel discomfort from the intrusion into her anus.

Anna's father, like many parents, was not aware that young babies would store memories of what happened in both their tissue and their brains. Trying to meet his own needs, he didn't know Anna was creating associations with her sexual energy that would remain with her until she was able to relinquish them with psychotherapy and the body work of Rolfing. (See Chapter 14 for more on Rolfing.) He didn't know his acts with her were a result of his cross-wiring from stored memories of his own, now automatic and unconscious.

Anna developed several forms of cross-wiring from incest. One was an association of intense sexual arousal with anal stimulation. While the anus is an erogenous zone and an area of the body that can contribute to sexual arousal, the kind of stimulation Anna experienced was of a different nature. In contrast to the opening, flowing arousal that people can allow to flood through their bodies, arousal from cross-wiring is intense, one-dimensional and driven. It feels like water under high pressure blowing out a hose, in contrast to gentle streams or magnificent rivers.

When Anna had sex she enjoyed all the activities, but she carried in her mind the knowledge that anal stimulation would occur. Focus on it intensified her arousal, and when the anal touch or penetration finally came she quickly reached orgasm. She used the knowledge that she would receive it to create an arousing suspense during the early part of sex. This effect was heightened by postponing anal stimulation, and she knew she must postpone it until she was ready for her orgasm, which for her meant the ending of that sexual encounter.

This particular cross-wiring created little difficulty for sexual relating. It wasn't illegal and didn't require Anna to violate her values. She became aware of the effect it was having when she entered a relationship in which she and her lover embarked on a course of examining all their sexual relating, as this book proposes we do to retrieve our sexual innocence. They agreed to focus on all feelings and patterns that came up during sexual activity as a way to educate themselves about what really happens during sex.

When Anna found that focusing her attention on her anus made her become unaware of her lover, she stopped the sexual activity and directed their attention onto her feelings. She discovered that suspense intensified arousal, and in the midst of those driven feelings she could no longer feel love for her partner. As Anna told Peter her feelings as they came up during sex, she gradually opened her awareness of what was happening and made connections between the driven arousal and losing awareness of him.

As she proceeded with this work, two important pieces of information became conscious. One, Anna began to have glimmers of memory that she had been sexually abused around her anus when she was too young to remember. This opened the door for her to use imagery and early sexual memory work to find out in detail what happened to her. She could then let go of the effects from unconscious memory.

Two, Anna learned what sex could be like without the driven feelings associated with anal stimulation. Anna had feared that without them she wouldn't experience much arousal and might become asexual. On the contrary, her sexual arousal became deeper and more satisfying. She was able to look at Peter and fully receive him. Their sexual energy became an exchange as his intensified hers and hers intensified his. They mapped out the paths that sexual energy took through their bodies and even felt as if their two bodies had melted together at their chests to become one. As they cleared away more and more of the inhibitors, Anna experienced having her lover more fully. The nature of her sexual arousal changed and steadily grew.

A second form of cross-wiring that had great impact on Anna had been created by her mother's unconscious awareness of the relationship between her husband and daughter. Her mother saw Anna as a competitor — which, by virtue of her father's choices, she was. She had all the anger at Anna that one feels toward a spouse's lover. This anger is dangerous to a young child who is dependent on parents for life itself. By preschool years Anna tried to become unattractive to her father so he wouldn't treat her as a little surrogate wife and trigger her mother's anger. It wasn't possible to say "no" to him, so the next best solution was not to attract him.

When Anna reached dating years she did not attract men. She believed they were not attracted to her because she was ugly. She didn't remember making the decision to avoid attracting men to her sexually. She was able to discount all evidence that she was an attractive woman and men would be drawn to her if she were to allow them to be. This view of herself as ugly remained until well into her recovery. She told me that when she was 43 and newly separated from her first husband, she didn't think of younger men as possibilities for dating. Yet many younger men, some in their early 20s, were asking her for dates and acting very interested. She was friendly and playful with these men and they were drawn to her vivaciousness. She hadn't hidden her likable qualities from them and of course they responded.

The unconscious decision to be plain and withdrawn so her father wouldn't see her resulted in Anna's belief that she was homely. At the same time she desperately wanted to be sexy, so she routinely bought clothes that showed off her body. Her mind figured she could be sexy to attract men even though she couldn't be attractive in other ways. But when she was the recipient of whistles or comments she felt enraged, reflecting her ambivalent needs. She also found it odd that when she saw pictures of herself she thought she looked wonderful. The pictures didn't match her beliefs or the reactions from men. This was all puzzling to her until she could unravel the roots of the cross-wiring.

Anna was the victim of a third form of cross-wiring. She turned off sexual feelings in her genitals in her attempt to avoid the critical, shaming look she received from her mother whenever she exhibited any sexual or romantic expression. Anna believes the looks started when she was very young and her mother would intuit her father's actions. The only way her mother knew to protect Anna from an "unknown" assailant was to monitor her behavior.

Anna fell in love with a man when in her late teens and decided to have intercourse with him. Although she felt passionate and romantic about him, when he touched her breasts or genitals she felt only a mild, nice feeling that she did not describe as sexual. Her body was able to prepare for intercourse by lubricating and changing texture, but for a year she didn't experience the strong arousal that builds and can impel orgasm. Anna was fortunate because the man with whom she began her sex life was gentle and undemanding. He enjoyed loving her even though she was not passionate in their sexual relating. Many women choose men who aren't able to be patient while they reclaim their sexuality, and this further encourages the unconscious decision to repress direct sexual feelings. Anna married a man who was gentle, and they explored sex together over many years. She began to enjoy sex and to have orgasms. During these years she discovered the power of anal stimulation.

Cross-wiring from incest can also connect sexual feeling to parts of the body that are not inherently sexual. Rick feels strong sexual arousal when his underarms are stimulated during sex. He believed underarms were erogenous zones for all people until his lovers convinced him it wasn't true. When he was able to uncover his childhood incest, he found that when he was a baby he was held by his underarms above his father's head as his father took his genitals into his mouth. The arousal of the genitals was associated with the intense feeling of having his weight supported under his arms. This body memory was useful in his recovery.

From Victim To Abuser: Replaying The Story

In my work as a psychotherapist specializing in sexuality I have the opportunity to view one of the most damaging effects of cross-wiring from incest. As my clients begin to trust me and allow themselves to be aware of their childhoods, they reveal more and more about what was done to them. As their memories become conscious and then spoken, they may also become conscious of the sexual child abuse they have committed. Once they are able to tolerate the shame that comes with such an admission, they are able to see the direct link between what was done to them and what they have done to others.

Carla had been in therapy with me for over a year when she became strong enough to face the sexual and emotional abuse that characterized her childhood. Memories flooded back in a period of weeks. With them came the awareness that she had sexually touched young boys she took care of as a teenager. The feelings she had when doing this were sexual, but also included feelings of power over another person. The children were smaller than she and couldn't defend themselves. Carla felt clever in getting them to cooperate without putting up a defense. She did this by telling them their parents weren't coming home until the next day and she was all they had. She also felt powerful seducing them with their own sexual feelings.

As we retraced Carla's childhood, we saw she was replaying her own experience but recasting herself in the role of the powerful one. Her father had enjoyed feelings of power over her and her mother through violating their sexual boundaries in a sadistic way. Memories unfolded as Carla talked about an incident when she and her teenage daughter were in the back seat of a car and her own parents were in the front. She saw her father reach around her mother's shoulder and grab her breast. Her mother pushed his hand away angrily. Carla was surprised when I told her that her father was sexually abusing all of them. He was physically violating his wife and creating emotional incest by forcing Carla and her daughter to experience this physical intrusion. Once Carla could see that his behavior was abusive, the door opened to a rush of memories from early years.

People who are sexually abused may act out the memory either in the form they experienced it or through taking the position of the person who abused them. The story can be replayed generation after generation until one person finds a listener who can translate the code and break the spell of the commandment, Thou Shalt Not Be Aware. (This is the title of Alice Miller's book on the cultural repression of awareness of child sexual abuse.) Only when we can become conscious of what happened to our sexuality can we tell the story, have the feelings we couldn't have before and let it go. Then we don't have to tell our story by re-enacting it with little children or other victims.

Seeing how we have perpetuated the abuse cycle is an excruciating part of the healing process. Much of our anxiety about retrieving memories is the fear that finding out the whole story would be unbearable. Our society condemns people who are sexual with children, and at the same time it supports child abuse by instilling secrecy around all sexual things. Methods we can use to heal from our own abuses, and thus not be in a position to reenact them with our children, are prohibited; and our cultural belief in the ownership of children only encourages their sexual use.

All of us who were sexually abused as children are trying to express that experience now, and we will continue until we have been able to tell the story with words and feelings. We are trained to repress awareness of what we are doing and have done. This training prohibits us from knowing that our neighbors are also abusing the sexual energy of children and adults — that we are not alone.

Rick's oldest brother sexually abused each of his four younger siblings into their preteen years. Rick hated him intensely. However, when Rick remembered that his father had sexually abused him from infancy we realized that his brother had been abused as well. His brother was trying to tell his story by acting it out with younger siblings. And his father was also acting out his own story.

I am sure I haven't retrieved all the ways I play out the abuse from my childhood. I know that when I was three and four I abused my sisters (then one and two) sexually. When I was in elementary school I played with dolls that were sexually violent with each other. These memories carried great shame, but are innocent compared with what is possible. When my son was a baby I worried about touching him in ways that might be sexual. (This was in 1970, long before the media began to frighten people about inappropriate touch.) Babies can perceive this discomfort, so he received messages about sexuality that contaminated him even though I was trying hard not to damage him. At the time I had no idea I had been abused and it never occurred to me that it was odd to be wondering if I was being sexual with him. I didn't understand the concept of natural sexual boundaries.

Nonincestuous Sexual Abuse

Babysitters, friends of siblings, other older children and adult sex addicts who are attracted to children are among those who abuse children sexually. The damage is usually not as great as that from incest and adults have less difficulty remembering these events and their feelings about them. While the abuse is harmful, of course, the complexity of feelings that are common in incest are less likely in a non-family situation.

One tragic reason for sexual abuse comes from curiosity of older children and adults about genitals. A seemingly natural way to satisfy this curiosity is to examine the genitals of younger children, especially those who are supposedly too young to know what is happening. If this were done without sexual energy, the person would be able to be curious in a way that would not convey shame and disgust to the child. The child could take pleasure in being seen as a whole, sexual creature and would not feel used. The shame and secrecy felt by older children or adults isolate them emotionally from the child they are touching. The child feels *objectified*, which is terrifying for someone who is totally dependent. The "badness" of the exploration, conveyed by the adult, introduces feelings of shame to the child. When the touch of genitals brings sexual arousal, the arousal becomes cross-wired with terror and shame. The child's sexuality is already becoming damaged.

Cross-Wiring From Relationships

A child's non-sexual relationships with parents and other relatives can also bring about cross-wiring of sexual energy. Harville Hendrix, in *Getting the Love You Want*, does an excellent job of connecting our childhood relationships with parents to our attraction to potential partners in adulthood. Some of this attraction is sexual even when no overt sexual behavior or sexualizing went on in childhood.

One example of sexual cross-wiring that can come from non-sexual relating is the association of love and sex. The intense, loving expression on a mother's face when looking at her young child is the same passionate look on the face of a lover. Children who didn't receive enough of their mother's loving looks retain the desire to find such looks in their adult lives. They are not able to outgrow it as a *need*, thereby allowing it to become a *delight* instead. As long as that look is experienced as a need, it becomes transferred onto sex partners as a need from them. Sex then takes on many more meanings than bonding, pleasure and spiritual awakening.

Bob, the man who was addicted to affairs as discussed in Chapter One, became addicted to adoring looks because of a dramatic deprivation. His mother, seriously depressed and addicted to alcohol, wasn't able to focus outward to meet his needs. His father left the family entirely and began a new life in which his son was not welcome. Since sexual looking is as intense as parental looking in infancy, Bob became smitten with infatuation. Normal developing relationships do not provide continual romantic looking, so he grew to feel unloved in each encounter. He married and then had a series of affairs as he searched for enough of this mother loving. Of course it wasn't possible to make up for the deprivation of love with sexual infatuation. He also had to contend with guilt and remorse for violating his marriage.

Bob's addiction is a form of a common phenomenon. Most of us find the intense look of a desired lover to be powerful proof that we are loved and safe, much as we did with our mothers when we were babies. In reality, such looks assist one function of sexual energy — bonding two people into a couple.

It is common for men, who as boys are typically turned away from maternal closeness sooner than girls, to search for that closeness through sex with a woman. The combination of wanting closeness and believing that it isn't forthcoming can result in a man's creating exactly what he expects. Men who have been in a relationship for a time can actually reduce their partner's interest in being sexual, thereby confirming that the proof of love isn't forthcoming. Feelings of rejection and anger that characterized the frustrated pursuit of mother, along with the social prescription to act like a man by not needing mother, become projected onto the partner. The partner may have tried in the beginning to meet this need from childhood, but after a time finds the task impossible.

Thomas believed his wife didn't want to have sex with him because he was a premature ejaculator, but once we delved into his sexual life we discovered this wasn't the case. He needed sex to feel loved and safe. He expressed this by silently pursuing her, constantly waiting for the moment she would give in. During the ten years of their marriage he always felt deprived and unlovable because of her resistance to his approach. As we talked, however, he remembered that before marriage she was very interested in sex but he didn't want to respond to her, fearing he couldn't "satisfy" her. No matter how often she had sex with him, it left him feeling inadequate. Thomas's affection-deprived relationship with his mother had become translated into an addictive use of sexual energy. A great deal of his attention was focused on whether or not he would receive sex — attention that could have been spent in more fruitful, pleasurable ways.

Emotional Incest

Triangulated relationships are a common source of cross-wiring that may or may not include overt incest. When triangulation occurs with a parent and one child, emotional incest co-exists. Examples of family triangulation are when a mother takes her son as a surrogate husband, or a father takes his daughter as a surrogate wife. The parent focuses on the child as the parent's primary relationship. An obvious symptom of a dysfunctional marriage, triangulation has effects similar to those of overt incest.

Triangulation between my father, my mother and me was a significant source of cross-wiring from my childhood. My mother intuitively but unconsciously knew that my father was not limiting his sexual energy to their marriage. As is commonly the case, she couldn't let herself know what was happening because knowledge would have required action. She can tell me now that if she had known she would have killed him. This rage had to go somewhere, so it was directed at the "other woman" — me. This didn't make sense to her either because I was only a baby, so she lived with seething rage with no outlet for it.

I perceived this rage and learned to avoid anything that would make it more intense. I hid any evidence of my sexuality even as a young child. I avoided all but the most superficial relating with my father. I grew up believing there was some dangerously powerful force associated with sexual feelings. I was truly surprised the first time I had sex to find that nothing changed. I didn't die and the world didn't end! My sexual activities couldn't have been what my mother feared. It was many more years before I understood that my sexuality was not the cause of her intense feelings.

As an adult I became vividly aware of the competition between women for "the man," and the feelings of power when chosen and feelings of worthlessness when cast into the role of the old, used-up one. Even though I was the chosen one, I always knew the other position — the one my mother had been in — was possible.

Triangulation in my childhood created strong feelings about love triangles in my adult life. I liked new relationships because I felt secure that my lover's attention was really on me. Once the relationship became stable, I found myself always on the alert for signs that his attention had moved to another woman. I didn't fear he would leave me but believed he would be untrue to me in some indirect way. And he was. They all were because of the particular training they had received in becoming males in our society.

Our culture expects men to look and lust, and they must respond to flirtation to feel like real men. Many men feel better about themselves when they engage in flirtations because it proves they are attractive enough to receive such attention. However, my raging response when I saw my partners flirting came from more than awareness that it wasn't a loving use of sexual energy. It came from being in the position in which my father had put my mother and me. One of us got to be the newly chosen center of attention, while the other had to be the neglected old used one.

Desiring relationships with married men is an obvious outcome of this cross-wiring. A woman may wish to be the new one, the one he feels intensely loving about, even though he is married to someone else he is probably not going to leave. When he does leave and marries the lover, the woman who has this cross-wiring will become jealous and possessive in the belief that he will do the same with her now that she is the old used, safe one. While there is some reality in this because of his past behavior, cross-wiring also causes these feelings.

I unwired these associations by forming a relationship with my husband, Rex, based on two commitments. First, we tell each other *everything*, even when we know it will bring on a strong reaction, and second, we agree to work steadily on reclaiming healthy sexual energy by examining every scrap of information. With his permission, I pointed out every time I saw women flirt with him and every time he responded, not knowing they were flirting. I held my fingers up by my face to indicate my "inner voices" were speaking and I "yelled" at him for wanting another woman more than me and seeing me as used goods, no longer attractive. Over time I became convinced that he wasn't doing this, and I also educated him about flirting and his response to it. He was not conscious of the flirtation coming his way because he had never believed he was worthy of it. Once he could see it then he could stop responding to it.

The work we have done together has allowed me to know I am part of a solid, monogamous, committed marriage and my husband does not see me as old, used up and discardable. On the contrary, he finds me powerful, loving and sexual and is delighted to be with me. This contradiction erased the belief that the way my father dealt with my mother and me is a pattern for the way all people will be with me.

The *fact* that Rex wasn't doing what my father had done was not enough to contradict my patterns. I also had to look and talk and have my feelings about it. Then I could stop replaying my childhood.

Antidotes To Shaming

The antidotes to individual, family and cultural shaming of sex are talking about sex openly, refusing to engage in shame-laced humor and refusing to shame our behaviors that aren't a loving use of sexual energy. As we refuse shame, we become open to the joyful, free, spontaneous — yet fully boundaried — expression of our sexual selves. We can know when it is appropriate to allow sexual unfolding and when it is not in the best interests of ourselves or another person (such as a child) to engage sexually. These awarenesses can be gentle and easy with absolutely no feelings of shame.

3

The Role Of Our
Culture

We Have All Been Sexually Abused

Our culture makes it impossible for any one of us to reach
adulthood with sexual health. We have all experienced sexual
abuse in some form. Abuse is not limited to forbidden touching.
Secrecy about sex and universal *shaming* of evidence of sexuality
are pervasively damaging to every one of us. These factors
have allowed all the overtly abusive things to take place, un-
noticed by our culture until the past two decades.

Sexuality in childhood is a secret business that we are forced
to figure out. We are not allowed to ask questions or otherwise
talk about our concerns. We are shamed by our entire culture,
including those who do not wish to shame us. This is abusive to
our growing sexuality. We adopt invisible cultural rules that
interfere with our sexuality and then pass them on to others
with no awareness of what we are doing. Until we can talk and

41

talk and talk about sex and our early sexual memories, this cultural ruling will continue, affecting all who cannot see it.

Alice Miller's book *Thou Shalt Not Be Aware* describes the psychological processes through which we repress our childhood memories of sexual abuse. Because of this repression we unavoidably pass on the same abuse to the next generation. In the afterword of the American edition she summarizes the understanding she reached in 1983:

> For millennia it has been *permissible and customary for children to be used to satisfy a wide variety of adult needs.* They have provided a cheap source of labor, an ideal outlet for the discharge of stored-up affect, a receptacle for unwanted feelings, an object for the projection of conflicts and fears, compensation for feelings of inferiority, and an opportunity for exercising power and obtaining pleasure. *Among all the different ways of misusing a child, sexual abuse is of particular significance, stemming as it does from the major role sexuality plays in our body and from the hypocrisy still surrounding it in our society.*
>
> Since beatings and tormenting, demeaning and humiliating treatment of children have always been regarded as forms of discipline "for their own good," these methods have been applied quite openly. There are still many people today who are fully in favor of child-rearing principles of this nature, and therefore child-beating can be widely observed, for it need not take place behind closed doors. This can lead to the fortunate circumstance that children find an adult witness who has the courage to come to their aid and defend them, for the adult knows how wounding this humiliating treatment is. Such support can help children perceive that a wrong has been done to them and thus make it possible for them to integrate this unhappy segment of reality into their lives. Then they will not have to spend the rest of their lives blaming themselves for what happened to them. But in the case of sexual abuse, which unlike beatings, usually takes place surreptitiously and under cover of darkness, the likelihood of finding the help of a courageous witness who can facilitate the integration of what happened is much slimmer. Children cannot achieve integration by themselves. They have no choice but to repress the experience, because the pain caused by their fear, isolation, betrayed expectation of receiving love, helplessness, and feelings of shame and guilt is unbearable. Further, the puzzling silence on the part of the adult and the contradiction between his deeds and the moral principles and prohibitions he proclaims by light of day create an intolerable confusion in the child that must be done away with by means of repression.

If older children who earlier had the good fortune to be able to trust their perceptions with their first attachment figure are sexually molested, they may be able to acknowledge the trauma and take it seriously, retain the memory of it, and with time work the experience through. If, however, this essential feature is missing, as it often is, and *if children are talked out of what they perceive, then the experience they undergo will later be seen in a diffuse, hazy light; its reality will remain uncertain and indistinct, laden with feelings of guilt and shame, and as adults these children either will know nothing of what happened or will question their memory of it.* This will be even more the case if the abuse occurred in early childhood. Since very young children do not find support within their own self or a mirror in the eyes of a witness, they must deny the truth. Later, the patient will *repeatedly and unconsciously reenact this reality, will tell the story by way of symptoms, including physical ones,* and will hope that the whole thing is only a matter of fantasy. (Emphasis added.)

When we reach adulthood sexual abuse appears in many forms of cross-wiring. The cross-wired sexual activities of adulthood tell the story of childhood incest. Thus these adult forms are a door into the past that allows us to retrieve some of the memories from repression. Examining sexual fantasies, pornography preferences and sexual interests that go beyond the unfolding of a bonding relationship can provide information about our childhood.

We All Use Sexual Energy Addictively

We live in a culture with values that promote addictive use of sexual energy. The focus on "outside-in" erotic stimulation prevents us from discovering our sexuality from the inside out. This emphasis is compounded by the blanket rule that we must not talk about sex, preventing us from learning truths that might help us understand our erotic nature. Each of us has to invent our own sex education, which is difficult to do with accuracy. We are more likely to be directed by cultural rules.

When we are children our brains aren't well developed, so we construct beliefs from data that we don't understand. For most things, such as food preparation and driving cars, we get to correct our original ideas as we grow older and our mature brains can better assemble the facts. But with sex it isn't so easy. As children we are shamed when we let our sexuality show, and we are told not to talk about it and to see it as entirely private. Of course we develop many very wrong ideas because we can't ask questions and gather information in an open way. Most of us don't get another chance to learn this secret business.

When we are ready for a mate, we match up with another person who also has erroneous childhood beliefs and who was also taught that sex mustn't be talked about. This enforces the cultural prescription not to talk and supports the effects of cross-wiring in the relationship.

As older children and adults we take in information from our cultural communicators — parents, schools, TV, movies, comic strips. I didn't have TV as a child, so I learned from the funnies and *Dear Abby*. Blondie and Dagwood showed me that women are the strong ones, but they must make men seem to be. L'il Abner made it clear that the right woman has large breasts and a small waist.

Learned Sexual Responses

Another way to look at cross-wiring of sexual energy is to talk about learned sexual responses. Most of our sexual responses are not inside-out emerging of arousal. Instead, they are conditioned by experiences and instruction we had as children and the cultural rules we absorbed as we grew up. We have learned that thin, young, large-breasted women, muscled men, nudity, flirtatious looks and "suggestive" remarks and movements are sexually arousing. In addition to the culturally-defined attributes, we each have our preferences as far as coloring, body type and personality. These have nothing to do with quality of interaction and serve only to limit our choice of partner. When we can undo our cross-wiring, we can select a person based on meaningful qualities and our sexual interest can emerge out of loving rather than out of socialization.

Our culture infuses itself into our interactions with others. We are not conscious of this process. To change the rules when we grow up, we must discern and examine the rules by which we operate and see what we can change.

One way to do this is to look at the "cross-wiring" of sexual energy with other human facets that have little to do with sex.

I am presenting 11 dominant rules here, but there are countless variations and idiosyncratic forms you can discover from your own cross-wiring.

Social/Sexual Rules Of Conduct

RULE 1. We Are Required To Have Sex If We Are In A Coupled Relationship.

A major rule of sexual behavior is that if we are married, we must engage in sexual activity with our partner. Many couples who come to me for help with their sexuality begin with the belief that there is something wrong with the person who doesn't want sex and that she or he must become sexual. This rule prevents both people from finding out why sexual energy isn't flowing and unfolding.

Anna came to me because her partner didn't feel loved by her when she didn't want sex. She wanted me to help her want sex. We quickly focused on the truth of *his* statement — she didn't love him. She was putting off the decision to end the relationship, and she no longer had sexual energy for it. Her belief that she must be sexual as long as they were a couple interfered with seeing the truth.

Her story provides examples of cross-wiring that come from a childhood in which sexual abuse influenced the child's views of sex. In her case safety in the world became intertwined with sexuality. The interrelationship between childhood and cultural beliefs prepared Anna for a dysfunctional marriage.

She couldn't say no to her father when he sexually abused her and used her as a surrogate wife. She believed saying yes was necessary because her young child's mind saw him as the source of safety, the strong person in the family without whom she would perish. Her mother seemed to depend on her father and didn't feel adequate to protect her.

Anna married a man who let her know that he would like to have sex at least every other day. He associated sex with love and needed reassurance from her that he was loved and wouldn't be abandoned. Anna did not feel loved by his desire for her, and over the years she grew less and less interested in having sex with him. *Yet she did anyway.*

We can see the role her childhood played in setting her up for this kind of sex life. At the same time her behavior was supported by our culture, which specifies that married people are to have sex with each other and are responsible for meeting the other person's "sexual needs." According to church and state, a couple isn't married until they have consummated the union with sex. If a person has an affair but can state that the spouse isn't making sex available, the need to get it somewhere else becomes an almost acceptable rationalization.

Anna dealt with a double-edged rule. Her automatic acquiescence to her father throughout her childhood carried over to her husband. At the same time another part of her knew that to have sex would be a further violation of herself because she would once again let herself be used for the needs of another person. She would participate in a lie by agreeing that the sex was an act of loving when it wasn't. She had no one to mirror this other part of her.

When Anna divorced her husband she believed she would not marry again. One reason was her desire never again to have sex unless she absolutely wanted it for herself. Over years of dating and daring to say no, she saw that she could marry *and* maintain her freedom of choice. Her second husband understands her reasons and agrees with her that neither of them must say yes when they want to say no. They have spent many months working on the various components of this cultural belief and probably have not yet put it entirely to rest. This view is deeply entrenched in our cultural view of marriage.

RULE 2. People Must Have Sex To Keep Their Partners At Home, And . . .

RULE 3. Those With Sexually Reluctant Partners Are Justified In Finding Sex Elsewhere.

A scene from the movie *The Men's Club* shows us a man who is addicted to brief affairs. He tells us that he goes from sex with another woman to a perfect house, perfect dinner and perfect family. When he remembers what he has just done, he finds himself criticizing the flowers on the table.

He rationalizes that his wife's reluctance to have sex justifies finding it elsewhere. She knows she must have sex to keep him at home. Our culture supports both these rules.

Women And Men — Two Ships In The Night

In another scene he pushes his sleeping wife onto her back, climbs on top of her and begins to pull her underpants off and put his penis in. She wakes up frightened and jumps out of bed, yelling at him to never do that again. We watch as her self-protective stance gives way out of guilt and fear. She apologizes, gets into bed, kisses him and tells him they will have sex tomorrow after she has had a good night's sleep. She lies to him.

We may assume that his rage at women was brought about by this very lying and reluctant sexual obligation, and by using him to get a house and money. He has created the situation that makes him feel used and deceived, proving once again "how women are." Neither of them understands the dynamics of their sex life and they don't know they can change it by telling each other the truth.

In the first half of the movie we learn each man's story about his sex life. We feel disgust after each. "Those *men!*" But they weren't born this way. Neither were you. Our culture prepares men to have anger toward women with no understanding of why it is there or what to do about it. Men are left dealing with guilt for having these feelings, and the only available culturally-supported method seems to be to cut off the feelings. Yet this results in other sexual behaviors that lead farther from a loving use of sexual energy and create even more need to distance oneself from the guilt and shame that results.

Herb Goldberg wrote a book aptly called *The Hazards of Being Male.* It can help both men and women to learn more about these crazy-making distortions of sexuality and the sex roles that our culture has implanted. Addiction is one of the few ways to adapt to these male-female cross purposes. Freeing yourself from the addictive use of sexual energy will require learning about these rules that keep men and women hating each other and promoting sexual addiction.

Women Are Seen As Violated, Men As Violators

Women are taught to be frigid. We have been shamed, ostensibly to protect us from sexual violation. A growing female child whose sexual feelings have been submerged will be safe from responding to men's sexual interest in her and thus from objectification as a sex object. In the cultural stereotype of unhealthy sexual energy, we are the victims.

Men, on the other hand, are seen as the violators. As children they are shamed for interest in their penises and the feelings that accompany them. Men are taught by cultural rules to *express* their shame-laced sexuality by "sowing their wild oats," conquering women and proving their masculinity with sexual prowess.

Women are taught to *withhold* shame-laced sexual feelings, converting them into "love and romance." Women who are openly sexual are considered to be bad. (This is changing in today's world, but slowly.) Women who have submerged their sexuality are considered to be normal, although inconvenient.

Promiscuity, impersonal sex, conversion of sex into love and romance, and shutting off sexuality are all violations of this powerful human capacity. Men and women are both violators and violated. The cultural view that only men are violators sets them up to feel like shameful persons and supports the solution of cutting the self off from feelings of shame. Once that is done a man cannot be aware of his partner and further violates himself and her.

The cultural view that women are violated sets them up to feel like victims, oppressed and abused. It also makes women blind to the way they support these views and the ways they confirm the view that they are eternally violated.

RULE 4. "Real Men" Are Good Lovers.

Another major cultural rule is that men must be good lovers, have an erection when they want and never turn down sex without a very good reason. In other words, men have vast performance requirements about how to be "real men." Being a real man is one of the basic elements of male self-esteem. The proverbial "locker room talk" about sexual prowess is based on this route to self-esteem. This need to show off is not conducive to real human sexual bonding. These cultural dictates prevent us from knowing the real function of sex and interfere with developing a relationship that can meet our needs for love and companionship.

The need to perform well is also the cause of most of the "sexual dysfunctions" treated by sex therapists. "Performing" inhibits us from learning about what is going on in our body and in our partner's body. That prevents us from directing our sexual activities in such a way that we can open ourselves to sexual energy. Having to perform blocks our awareness and it cannot flow in synchronization with our partner's sexuality.

"Sex by numbers" is the opposite of lovemaking. *Taking responsibility for another's orgasm* is a lot of work. *Not being able to stop sexual activity* once we have started feels entrapping and limiting. *Keeping an erection* regardless of how we feel is impossible. *Holding back orgasms* to keep our partner from being angry requires incredible self-discipline and breeds resentment. *Needing to control lovemaking* (if you can call it that) often emerges as a solution to the performance requirements, but then our desire to control is criticized.

Greg came to me for therapy because he couldn't maintain his erection when beginning intercourse. After eight years of marriage and *never* losing his erection, the one time he did was frightening. He believed something was wrong with him. This led to intense fear emerging every time he began intercourse, and the fear inevitably interfered with his arousal. The resulting loss of erection frightened him further and further decreased his ability to maintain his arousal and erection.

His wife was afraid that he didn't love her, that he was having an affair or that she wasn't attractive to him anymore. She needed him to have sex with her so she could feel like a whole woman. He believed the only way to reassure her was to have intercourse with her. This added further pressure and further inhibited the very erection that seemed necessary for her reassurance.

Many of the millions of men who seek impersonal sex in massage parlors and other places are seeking respite from the internalized demand to perform well. There are no rules about how you have to be with a prostitute. Healthy use of sexual energy requires that rules and other internalized cultural beliefs be abandoned at home, replaced by *unfolding* each sexual exchange. Sexual services for a fee would decline if men and women were able to create each sexual encounter with no prescriptions.

A friend who is working on his confusion about sex gave me his stream-of-conscious writing. I have excerpted some of it here.

> Where's the rule book, how do I do this? Oh performance, can I keep it up, will I come too soon?
> But then what if I do it too well and you will want to consume me and smother me? Be careful, don't look at her, don't be too open.

(To his partner.) My fears say you don't like sex, you want something from me. You don't really love me, you just want something. You are disgusted by me, and my penis is disgusting. It's dirty and smelly and you think I want to control you with it.

Then they say you like sex and all you want to do is use me. You just want a hard penis to do what you want with. All I am is a hard penis to you, a servant, your gigolo.

If you are a woman who feels you *have to have sex to be in a relationship* then you are supporting the ideas my friend is expressing. Women have been sexual when they don't want to and have lied to men. Men know this, of course. We all know at some level when we are being lied to. Then men don't trust that women *ever* really want to have sex or make love with them. A man can only trust his partner when he knows on all levels that she is being truthful with him. When he knows this, he can believe that she truly wants sex when she indicates she does. And even in this kind of relationship they will have to overcome the cultural rules that have led men to hate women.

Continuing with my friend's writing:

Men are disgusting. "Men," my mother said with disgust. So I didn't want to be a man. Yet at the same time, a man is defined by how hard his cock is. So you don't have any of your feelings. It's easier for a woman to become just a sex object and you just a machine.

If I put my hand on your breast, you would think it was inappropriate — and a lot of men before me were inappropriate because they have shut off their feelings to live up to the requirements. So why should you trust me? And I have shut off my feelings, too, and created a lot of distrust. I touched breasts when I didn't see the rest of the woman, and then when they objected I thought it was me they didn't like. But I couldn't look at the whole woman, it was too frightening to see her. She might be seeing me the way my mother saw men. She might not know I am not one of *those* men — but there I was acting just like one because I was afraid of her reactions. And now that I am ready to see all of you, I'm afraid it's too late.

Men excuse their behavior by saying their penis doesn't have a conscience. It controls them. This means they can't be trusted about anything sexual. If you believe this, then you shouldn't trust me. I don't want to be one of them but I am born with a penis. And I like my penis. I don't want to abandon it because women won't trust me with it. I do have a conscience about my sexuality, and I want you to know it. If I shut down when we are sexual, it is because of all the fear from years of training. See past it. I am not how my mother said men are.

I set it up so you come after me because that will mean you really care for me and love me. But you feel that I don't really want sex. If I pursue you, I am sure you will find my sexual feelings and wanting of you disgusting and inappropriate. But if you pursue, then my performance stuff comes up. I have to do it right, just the way you want it. So I want to pursue, but if I do then I can't believe you are really loving me. I have to do it as long as you want because if I don't I am less than a man. I am only as valuable as I am able to perform.

If I come before you do, then you will think sex is over and I won't want to be involved with your orgasm. You think sex is disgusting for me if I don't get aroused again. I assume you are pissed off and disappointed because the only way you can have any pleasure is if I have an erection. When we do continue to be sexual, I am amazed that you still want to be sexual.

Then there are the times when I think you want to just suck me up into you through your vagina. I feel like I'll never be my own person again, I'll be lost. Even though sometimes when our bodies seem to melt into one it feels so incredible, and I want to do it again and again. But then I don't want to have sex, and then I think I should because men do.

I can't touch your breast when we aren't having sex because I think it will be disgusting to you. I don't know when you will be receptive, even though I know you so well in all other ways. I am very sensitive to your moods and what your body communicates when we hug. I know when you want to be hugged and when you don't. But I lose that ability to know when I reach out to touch your breast. My feelings get shut off, and then it proves to you that I am not open to your needs and feelings. And so it is just easier to not have sex. Or to space out and leave you when we do. But I have lost the ability to do that. Our relationship has become too real because we talk about everything and know each other so well. You'd think that if I knew you so well, I would with sex too, but it is harder with sex. And since I haven't explained these things to you, then you don't know me either. So let's just not have sex!

But that's not an option. I want to be sexual with you. I love you and I am spending my life with you. And when these voices are quiet, the sexual loving is something I have never known.

To reclaim healthy sexual energy we can become conscious of each rule that dominates sexual expression, examine it, let the "inner voices" speak and release them. Approach sexual relating as if it were a classroom — the task is to learn all you can about yourself, your partner and the rules that control you. You can give up the rules about how sex will go: the order of activities, the need for orgasms and the requirement that once you start you can't stop. Instead, *stop sex at any point* if a feeling comes up or a rule becomes apparent. Examining the rule to make it more conscious, and having the feelings that come with the rule and with breaking it, are the tools for letting it go. Chapters 10 and 12 will give you a more detailed description of how to accomplish these tasks.

RULE 5. We Must Have "Sexy" Bodies And "Good-Looking" Faces.

The idea that body parts and looks are naturally sexually arousing is so deeply entrenched that I get arguments when I say it is entirely dictated by culture. I would like to suggest that *any external stimulation of sexual energy is opposed to the inside-out, natural variety.* If we respond to body parts, pictures and "sexiness," we will inhibit inside-out sexual unfolding. It is also inhibited by seducing or being seduced, wearing alluring clothes or creating romance to "get in the mood." These are attempts to *override an inhibition about sex* so we can be sexual. Instead of helping two people love each other with sex, external stimulation promotes the very dynamics that encourage the addictive use of sexual energy.

My husband Rex and I have "unwired" our social training about sexy bodies and good-looking faces. We didn't focus directly on these patterns, but they changed along with those we intended to remove. For a long time Rex, who Rolfs bodies as one of his art forms, had been telling me that he didn't see glamorous women as sexy and instead was more attentive to the structure of bodies from his Rolfing eye. He uses his skills to bring bodies into alignment, and to him attractive bodies are those that are straight, agile and balanced. Attractive faces express a whole person whether or not they have makeup. In the beginning I had a hard time believing him because my inner voices were sure he was merely reassuring me that he could love my fat and wrinkles.

Seeing the movie *The Men's Club*, in which six men spend the second half of the movie having sex with a number of prostitutes, convinced me that he had actually "unwired" his sexual responsiveness to certain body types because I found that mine were now unwired as well. For two years we had examined every rule that dominated our sexual feelings, responding to the natural healthy sexual energy that emerged as the rules fell away. The unexpected benefit was that we also eliminated the rules about body types and overt sexual activity.

I can now see why he smiles when he looks at me while I'm in the bathtub with wet hair and my fat bunched up. My body is straight, agile and balanced because I have responded well to Rolfing and other forms of body work. My face is expressive of who is inside. And Rex loves me. This is the most important part. I am his chosen mate and he uses his sexual energy to bond with me into a loving partnership. The intimacy we have developed from constant, total honesty makes me the most beautiful person in the world to him, and no body or face can hold the interest that mine does. It makes no difference where I would rate in a competition with other women, because *with love bonding there is no competition*. There are no criteria with which to compare me to others.

If we truly love and believe the purpose of sex is to connect intimately with this person with whom we share life, then we will experience our lover's body as the most beautiful body there is. Our culture expects us to lust after "sexy" strangers and somehow still love our partner as she ages, becomes pregnant, changes weight and goes through menopause. If we believe our cultural rule about looks, then we must struggle with how to love our partner without reservation and feel unreservedly lovable.

Confusion Of Sexuality And Worth

Our culture defines human worth as one's rank on a number of attributes, including education, income, lifestyle and achievements. High on this list are attractiveness and sexiness as measured on the EMPA (Externally Measured Physical Attractiveness) scale. We are worth more in the eyes of our culture if we have qualities that the rest of us have been conditioned to believe are sexy. The irony is that all of us are potentially sexy and desirable to one who loves us. Acculturated beliefs interfere with natural love bonding.

Confusion arises when two people couple. Limiting sexuality to one other person also limits the resources for achieving outside-in self-esteem that comes from attracting other people sexually. If we feel good about ourself because people are sexually attracted to us, then when we couple we will have to make a choice. Either we give up that form of input or we flirt with others when our partner isn't present. Even if we give up flirting as a way to feel valuable, others around us will be making a case for the value of being sexually attractive (thin, dressed in style, groomed and well made-up) because it is built into our culture. It is difficult to accept ourself as perfectly beautiful and sexually luscious if we have extra pounds and the wrinkles of aging. Our cultural values make it difficult for other people to see us this way, too.

RULE 6. Flirting Is "Innocent."

Our culture supports the ooze of sexual energy over those who are not one's partner or potential partner. Advertising based on arousing sexual energy is one clear example of sexual stimulation that spills out in a socially acceptable form. Flirting by some salespeople, co-workers and bar patrons is so commonplace that few people recognize it as sexual. The lack of clear sexual boundaries in most people and the cultural acceptance of the sexual oozing make it difficult to know when we aren't using sexual energy in a healthy way.

Our culture (and probably our family) gives us two messages about flirtations. On the one hand we are rewarded for being cute and intense in a stylized way. We know we are valuable if we look like the latest idols and interact as they do. Some people pay more attention to us if we became skilled at talking and looking at them with sexualized interest. On the other hand we are criticized for paying too much attention to someone other than our partner. Our cultural rules make it impossible to do it right.

As we heal from these rules jealousy becomes an important source of information. It is a cue that something is going on that may look "normal" within our culture's definition, but is actually an unhealthy use of sexual energy. Our partner's jealousy might be a patterned reaction from childhood; it may also be a natural reaction to our use of flirtation to make life seem richer and to increase outside-in self-esteem. Our own jealousy may stem from childhood or indicate our partner is using sexual energy in ways that detract from our primary bond. As with most feelings, jealousy can be a powerful indicator of an area to which we may dedicate some recovery.

Triangulation with parents is a common backdrop for both flirting and jealousy from flirting. As my father's focus shifted from me to my mother and back to me, we took turns feeling powerful and feeling hatefully jealous of the other. One of us won and the other lost at all times. When I reached adulthood I wanted a man no other woman would want so I wouldn't have to compete for him. I also valued being in the position of the "other woman" because then I was the perpetual winner; the wife or primary partner was the loser.

As I was playing out these patterned behaviors, no one (except for those who moralize) suggested there was anything wrong with them. The socially acceptable rationalizations such as "we accidentally fell in love" or "this was something too special to pass up" were not only accepted but were suggested to me.

For an hour or so after my wedding ceremony with Rex I felt depressed. I was now the wife and again in the vulnerable position. He no longer had to pursue me and win me, and I feared his attention would stray elsewhere. These feelings gave me the opportunity to work through my history because I also knew Rex did not compare me to other women and he was committed to creating our relationship. As a result I embarked on a healing path that resulted in the complete absence of jealousy. This required a willingness both to examine my childhood with the feelings engendered there and to interact in honesty with Rex long enough so I could no longer believe he really wanted someone else. If he had been a flirtatious triangulator my patterns would have persisted because our relationship would not have offered a contradiction.

RULE 7. Sex Is Love.

Our social rules say sex is lovemaking. At the same time sex is used in advertising to sell products and is used to create outside-in feelings of worth in ways that have nothing to do with love. We are supposed to prove love with sex and to interpret sexual interest to mean we are loved. Our social rules contradict each other.

People who live with sex addicts are particularly vulnerable to this rule. When the addict uses prostitutes or pornography or masturbates compulsively, the partner often feels unloved and believes the addict is being unfaithful. If sex is love, this would be true. The addict, however, is having an experience more like the alcoholic under the influence of alcohol — he or she has entered an altered state of consciousness in which the concept of love has been obscured. *Most addictive acts have nothing to do with the partner and instead reflect the addict's desire to avoid reality.* This is also true when addicts want to "romance" their lovers and "make love" as one of the addictive activities.

Sex and love can be intimately intertwined in the healthy use of sexual energy. Sex is one powerful way to pull down barriers and allow two people to know each other fully. Yet sex is not automatically loving; it is only a tool that can allow loving to unfold.

The following scenario is based on a number of couples in therapy. It illustrates how a couple's relationship can be led into difficulties by the confusion of love and sex, accompanied by the rule that they cannot discuss sex.

Two people begin a relationship based on intense sexual attraction and thoroughly enjoy having sex with each other. Each feels deeply loved by the other, and life is enhanced. Then one day one person doesn't feel sexual. He has been under a great deal of stress at work which results in reduced interest in sex. His first impulse is to hide this from his partner so she won't think his feelings have changed. This is difficult, however, because a penis often won't cooperate.

At first he tries to reassure her, bringing flowers and saying how much he loves her. She enjoys this but at the same time finds herself suspicious about why he is being so attentive when he doesn't want to have sex, which to her is the only real measure of his love. So she pulls back, protecting herself from rejection. This in turn scares him, bringing up fears that he will lose her if he can't prove his love. So he does what he can to create an erection. He buys pornographic magazines and finds that by looking at them he can forget work and focus totally on his arousal. Praying to hold onto the arousal, he finds her and initiates sex. This works for a time, but he finds he has to have many different pictures and then create fantasies. The fantasies have to be of unusual practices to continue to arouse him.

One day she happens to look for something where he keeps the magazines and is shocked to find them. She thinks he really loves her, which, of course, he does. But she believes that if love equals sex, he would never look at another woman, and that would include pictures. She is sick at the thought that he has been aroused by these pictures and then has made love to her. She doesn't mention her find because she feels guilty for invading his privacy. But now she finds it difficult to receive his sexual advances. For a time she fakes arousal, but eventually she finds it easier to have a headache or be tired. She doesn't understand that finding the pictures and assuming that her husband doesn't love her results in the loss of her sexual interest. She assumes there is something wrong with her. She also fears she doesn't love him any more or that she is homosexual.

As sex wanes they both feel unloved, and these feelings permeate the rest of their relationship. They fight more and each find other people interesting in a sexually tinged way. This stirs up jealousy on both sides, but neither feels they have a right to object. Eventually they go into marriage counseling with a set of vague complaints.

If this couple had not assumed that sexual interest meant they were loved, *or* had they been able to discuss sex, they would not have experienced the predictable sequence of events. This composite of stories reflects the tragedy of our culture's rules.

The association between sex and love begins in childhood for those who are involved in any kind of incest. Contact with genitals and non-genital triangulation of the child with the parents can create associations of sexual energy with love and affection. If we are able to *see* what happened, *talk* about it and *heal* from it, then we can relinquish this association in the present. But this doesn't happen because our culture has rules that prohibit it. We mustn't see how the connections were formed, so of course we aren't able to heal from the effects. This is compounded by the cultural belief that love and sex are intertwined, which supports the understanding we created as children.

RULE 8. Romance Has Value.

Our culture has institutionalized the idea that romance is a necessary and valuable part of sexual loving. Women will often say that when they aren't in the mood for sex they can become ready if their partner will only be more romantic. A man is valued if he is romantic.

Romance is the creation of illusion, taking a couple away from loving intimacy. Flowers and candy, candlelight dinners, gifts and cards are all indirect communications that the rela-

tionship is important, and they often serve *to avoid the unfolding of real loving.*
Socialization of women includes the misdirection of sexual energy into romance. A woman is supposed to be swept off her feet by her lover, but not in a directly sexual way. Her sexual energy is to be engaged in a general kind of aroused state. Prior to the sexual revolution in the 60s, after which it became permissible for women to enjoy sex, the sexual energy that fuels couple bonding took the form of romance as much as genital sexual arousal.

You may be using the word "romantic" to mean affection and tenderness if you perceive the lack of such feelings in your partner. Women who have told me they need more romance are sometimes responding to their partner's emotional absence. For people who want to use sex lovingly, it isn't inviting to open sexually to a person who wants to use sex impersonally. But romance — the illusion of closeness — isn't the answer. Women have said they want flowers or a simple card, but when these are forthcoming their feelings of not being loved don't change.

Our cultural valuing of romance makes it easy for a person to become addicted to the accompanying feelings of euphoria. The quantities of romance novels that are published each year imply the extent of this addiction. Books and fantasy rarely include overt sexual acts, focusing instead on the feelings of love and bonding created by sexual energy. The early phases of my own sex addiction did not include sex itself, even though my body was swept with sexual feeling.

RULE 9. We Must Be Monogamous.

Our Judeo-Christian heritage dictates that when two people enter into marriage they will have no sexual interaction with others. This culturally sanctioned rule seems to protect each person from feelings of betrayal and is intended to protect the relationship from dissolution. Most people subscribe to this rule because of fear of the consequences if they were to break it. At the same time, most married people have sex with others during their marriages.

While I believe that healthy sexual energy includes a lasting, exclusive bond with a partner, I also believe this cannot occur if a couple is accepting the outside-in rule that they must be monogamous. Following a rule — which is a form of illusion — will prevent you from learning from the inside out the very real reasons why *you* want to be monogamous.

RULE 10. We Have To Satisfy A Sex Drive.

We grow into adulthood with the belief that men, and perhaps women, have a sex drive that must be satisfied. I believe this stems from the experience of adolescence during which sexual energy seems to emerge without stimulation and is quieted by orgasm. After years of repression and shaming, the hormones of puberty bring our sexuality out full blast, and it can feel uncontrollable. Men have told me about having erections during adolescence that made no sense, when they were standing in front of a classroom giving a speech, riding a bike, etc. They were not having sexual feelings, but erections occurred anyway.

Girls have corresponding clitoral erection but have been so-cialized to transform sexual feelings into erotic fantasy and "crushes." Our culture doesn't prepare us to evolve through this period and into a more mature experience of sexual energy.

We do not have a sex drive. We have sexual potential. We live in a society in which we have been conditioned to respond to certain stimuli as sexual. We are bombarded by these stimuli through advertising and by people who are seeking outside-in self-esteem by stimulating us. This combination of events makes us feel as if we have a sex drive. When we are able to undo social cross-wiring, it becomes possible to be aware of sexual energy floating through our bodies, to set it aside if attention is needed elsewhere and to choose when the time is right for expression. Many adults can attest that long periods of celibacy are quite comfortable and valuable.

RULE 11. Don't Talk About Sex.

The rule that we cannot talk about sex in an open, genuine way is the primary cultural influence that prevents us from changing our inhibiting rules. When we can bring sex into everyday conversation our world will be able to heal from the damage that centuries of silence have created.

One reason we have been silent about sex is to create boundaries around this important, potentially disruptive energy so it becomes manageable. While we need these boundaries, silence is not a useful way to create them. It backfires because it allows distortions of sexual energy to continue unchecked, generation after generation. It is our task to bring sex into the realm of ordinary life, to find out what boundaries are actually necessary and to learn how to establish them in a way that doesn't conflict with a full use of sexual energy.

A second reason for silence comes from the shame surrounding sex. As each generation reacts with shame to the sexuality of the next, these feelings are internalized and passed on to the following generation. Silence conveys shame and shame breeds silence.

The antidote to the association of sex with shame is to *talk* and *talk* and *talk* about sexuality, sexual feelings and sex itself. We need to replace the locker-room talk and bar talk that has perpetuated sexual distortion with serious conversation in safe places about real feelings and experiences.

(There is an exception to talking about explicit sex. In the early part of recovery hearing someone discuss sexual activity may trigger lust. It is important to limit sexual discussion when an early recoverer is present. If you are in the early stages of recovery and do not want to trigger your addiction, then it is essential that you set this boundary. You can, however, talk in general terms about your activities that feel shameful. This will begin the de-shaming process, which in turn will reduce your reaction to hearing sexually explicit discussion.)

Our Culture Inhibits Inside-Out Sexual Relating

Sex that emerges from the inside of a person or the inside of a relationship is a rich expression of humanness. We are capable of knowing when sex can enhance life and let our sexual energy emerge. Sex is part of life, a way of being that we can flow into and out of and still feel like ourselves.

By contrast, we live in a society which stimulates intense sexual interest from the outside with no consideration of its appropriateness for the individual. Most magazine ads and television shows try to grab our attention with sexual stimuli. A walk through a video store presents us with a variety of sexual scenes on the covers of movie cassettes. Some pictures are not overtly sexual, yet they resemble sex scenes. I studied the pictures on the boxes of workout videos, finding many designed to make one think sexually.

The effect of such stimulation is to train people to respond sexually to bodies and body positions. Some mothers fear their daughters are being violated by being seen as sex objects, but their only recourse is the same one taught by their mothers — to avoid sexual objectification by hiding one's body. At the same time, it is important for a daughter to be attractive to men to lead a normal life. Each of us has to figure out how to be sexually attractive without looking like "one of those women" — an impossible task. In the years when I aspired to this task my sexual awareness was pulled outside myself and outside of my body, even in my fantasies.

Men are supposed to respond positively to sexual attention from women in or outside of a love relationship. Men are also required to respond to body parts. A male is consequently pulled away from his own sexuality as it exists within, and he learns to use those external stimuli to pull up sexual arousal. His socialization as a man prevents him from knowing the warm, gentle and sometimes passionate experience of being a sexual person.

Toward Sexual Energy From The Inside Out

We can reverse our acculturated spiral toward impersonal, outside-in sexual energy (addiction). We can move toward inside-out sexual energy that comes from within the person and within the couple (natural).

There is an important implication to this process. *If we want to have unfolding, bonding, natural sex, it is necessary to relinquish all addictive uses of sexual energy.* As with all addictions, if we operate in the addiction we will move farther away from operating out of addiction. As the spiral is reversed and we become more in touch with the natural use of sexual energy, we will continue naturally to become ever more in touch with it. A writer in the book *Sexaholics Anonymous* said he wished he could "lust like a gentleman," the equivalent of social drinking to an alcoholic. For any of us, sex addicts or not, as we fully uncover our healthy sexual energy we will discover that we no longer lust at all.

This means we will find ourselves no longer responding to our addictive stimulators, *or to any outside-in stimulators.* Sexual response or interest evoked by pictures, movies, flirting or nudity will fall away, and we will find sex to be entirely of a different order. I have found that as I heal, sex becomes less and less important and more and more wonderful.

Creating A New Sub-Culture

Those of us who are healing from our socialized addictions are *creating a new culture,* or at present a sub-culture. We are learning that flirting doesn't serve our relationships, that we can eat what our bodies need and that the feelings we previously numbed with addictive maneuvers can emerge. We are examining the co-dependency that dominates human interaction so we can stop these confusing, unhealthy exchanges. We are learning step by step what it is to live in integrity and honesty. We are dedicated to uncovering our full selves and living richly. As this process evolves, we become less and less a part of the dominant culture and more like aliens who look curiously at what is going on here on Earth.

4

The Influence Of
Our Adult
Sex Life

Dating, marriage and interacting sexually all create a complex environment as we move into the years when sexual energy fuels our relationships. The effects of cultural prescriptions and the influence of our particular childhoods are compounded by the fact that both partners bring individual histories of abuse to a relationship. The result is that many adult relationships continue early abuses, seeming to confirm that sexual energy cannot be used in a healthy, life-enriching way.

In this chapter we will look at some of the ways our cultural views about relationships set us up to abuse each other and allow ourselves to be abused. The rules of "dating," repeated rejection, finding that our partner is not interested in sex with us and impersonal, objectifying sex are only some of the experiences we hear our friends talk about routinely.

We All Abuse Each Other

Given that we and our lovers have both been sexually abused in some fashion, are allowed to discuss sex in only a cursory manner, have developed incorrect associations for the meaning and purpose of sex, and are bombarded by erroneous messages from other people and the media — how can we expect to be able to use sex well? Add to this the reality that each of us is trying to meet needs in the relationship that we have misplaced. It is easy to see why hurt feelings, disappointments and anger are commonplace. No one escapes.

We all hurt each other, even when we try not to, because as we grew up our sexual energy was hurt. These hurts have taken many forms and so will their expression from the dating years into adulthood.

The Dating Years

Our adult sex life begins when we "date." Dating differs in a number of ways from spending intimate time with friends. We dress up to show ourselves off positively. We withhold information that might make the other person "like" us less. This is the opposite of revealing ourselves so the other person can really know us and we can really know them — the definition of intimacy.

The sexual rules of our culture influence dating and determine our personal status through such arbitrary judgments as who we date, how far we got, the amount of romance, how much he spent, where he took us, the kind of car he drives, how she dressed, the size of her breasts, etc.

Dating is not very healthy for love relationships. The alternative is to develop good friendships first and consciously decide to add sex only when it is time to bond. This approach can allow us to begin coupling more honestly. The reality is that our adult sex lives get off to a difficult start, often fraught by rejection from lovers or potential lovers.

Rejection Is Never Easy

Repeated rejections in relationships can create a belief (or support a belief created in childhood) that we are not valuable to others. Our culture defines a large part of our worth as our ability to attract people sexually and enter satisfactory relationships. People who cannot find partners or are rejected by their partners suffer from feelings of alienation and shame. I have had a number of women clients who had perfect looks by our culture's standards and had learned how to dress and make themselves up attractively. Yet the men in their lives could not remain in relationships with them. I am struck by the irony of the cultural view that these women "had it all" when they were leading miserable lives and were sometimes suicidal.

The ending of relationships is a normal part of the process of jostling around until pairs have been formed. A post-puberty trial and error period is necessary as young people find out what is important to them. This time becomes fraught with pain, however, because of the connection we have made between our personal worth and the desire expressed by a lover. The loss of a partner also reawakens the fear of abandonment from early childhood instead of being perceived as merely one attempt gone awry.

When Our Partner Does Not Want To Be Sexual

The absence of sexual interest or arousal, when it cannot be discussed, is traumatic for the other partner. I have seen many situations in which the person who is sexually turned down feels intensely abandoned and unloved because he or she places a certain value on sexual responsiveness. Such people come to me with their list of rules, asking me to confirm that the other person is wronging them. Their distress is very real.

Jackie called to make an appointment for marriage counseling because from the time they were married Matt had little interest in having sex with her. I learned later that he masturbated almost daily. As Jackie told me about their years together, the intensity of her frustration was apparent. She felt unattractive, unloved and as if something were very wrong with their relationship. She believed it was her fault. Our cultural beliefs support her assumptions.

As Matt and I talked alone, we began to see some of his cross-wiring. He felt guilty about sex because of shaming from his childhood. The feelings of guilt came up when he was with a woman he loved and prevented him from becoming aroused. His solution, common in our shame-based society, was to overpower the guilt feelings with outside-in stimulation. For Matt this required a new lover and sex practices he considered outside the norm. He was able to fantasize about these situations and arouse himself sufficiently to masturbate, so this became his preferred sex life. He wasn't interested in affairs. He loved his wife, enjoyed their relationship and had no interest in other women.

Our work centered on the causes of guilt and shame and on the cross-wiring so he could reclaim his natural sexuality and express it with his wife.

The work with Jackie took a different form. We looked at her culturally laden beliefs, especially the need to be sexually attractive to her husband to feel like a satisfactory person. Part of her rejected feelings were dispelled by understanding the reasons for her husband's lack of interest. She came to see that it was not based on her shortcomings. The rest required addressing her own culturally induced cross-wiring regarding sexual interest.

Check out your reactions to the two people I have described. Who seems to be the wronged party? Who is the abuser? Our socialization says the man is the abuser if he doesn't want sex with his wife and also if he wants it when she doesn't. See if your feelings change when I turn the sexes around.

Jean never wanted sex with her husband, and George was distraught over this. He tried everything. He was romantic, he bought her a vibrator and he watched to see when she seemed "in the mood." He felt unloved. He didn't know and couldn't understand that her feelings came from her fear of sex that started when she was sexually abused as a child. He sent her to therapy to find out why she didn't want sex, although he was afraid it was because she didn't love him.

Who is the abuser here? The wronged party?

My own socialization blinded me for a time to my sex-role stereotyping. In the past I would have sympathized with Jackie and criticized Matt for using fantasy and masturbation instead of having a sex life with her, and I would have felt that Jean's husband should be more understanding. I became conscious of what I was doing by hearing the stories of many men and finding out what it felt like to be in their shoes. I learned that both men and women feel distressed over their partner's lack of sexual interest.

Blaming The Other Person

As relationships evolve sexual humiliation may become common. It may include disparaging remarks about penis size, the ability to maintain erection or body features that are considered sexually unattractive. These remarks reflect the insecurity or other feelings of those who make them. Projecting "blame" onto the other person provides relief from feeling responsible for sexual difficulties. For example, a man who doesn't respond sexually to his wife because of deep fears about sex may find it less distressing to think the fault is hers because she isn't attractive enough to stimulate him. Women will often accept this kind of blame because we are socialized to believe we must have sexually attractive bodies to have a man. In this situation he is abused by the rule that he must always achieve an erection to be a real man, and she is abused by the belief that she is not an attractive woman if he doesn't want her sexually.

Partners As Objects

Making objects of sex partners is common in our sexually repressed society. We can set aside some of our cross-wired issues if we think of our partner as just a body with body parts that are useful to the sexual act. We can avoid fear of intimacy, fear of sex, feelings of shame and stored-up anger by not seeing who our partner really is. While objectifying is adaptive for the person who is doing it, the effect is quite abusive for the partner who is not able to see it.

A good friend I will call Karen speaks of her fear of being seen as a sex object by her husband. Jack has fears from his childhood experience of having his sexuality shamed, and he handles those fears by shutting off his consciousness when he begins to be sexual. As he objectifies Karen to accomplish this, she is not being loved by him. Since this isn't good for her she has stopped having sex with him for the present. At the same time she is aware that her own experiences of being used as a sex object when she was very young are re-awakened by Jack's emotional "disappearance" when he becomes sexual. Her healing involves working on her own history *and* giving her husband information about the effect he has on her. This will give him input so he can become aware of changes he can make.

Making Sex Impersonal

The abuse Jackie experienced was twofold. Her cross-wiring resulted in misinterpretation of her husband's actions as lack of interest; the solution to this was to address her own issues. At the same time another abuse was taking place. Matt's discomfort with conscious sexuality resulted in his depersonalizing sex. His need to fantasize that another woman was in bed with him and another activity was occurring kept him from being with Jackie. Even though she was not conscious of his absence, she could feel (as we all can in such situations) that he wasn't with her.

Both Matt and Jackie were living a lie that was called making love. Living lies, particularly about areas that are intimate, creates alienation and loneliness. People who have impersonal sex only increase their separation from others, even though their desire is to increase intimacy. When the actual route to intimacy is closed off by guilt, shame and fear, the imitation provided by impersonal sex seems to be positive. But it backfires by creating more distance. This is followed by a stronger urgency for closeness, again only possible with an imitation of intimacy, creating even more distance.

Relating With Physical Abuse

Rape in adulthood is a sexual abuse that creates intense cross-wiring of sexual energy with fear of further violation. Many of the same feelings experienced through sexual abuse in childhood show up for adult rape victims. A particularly devastating, culturally-encouraged effect is the belief that the victim is to blame.

Physically abusive relationships, even if rape isn't present, can result in the fear of sex. When others violate our physical beings we become afraid to open ourselves both sexually and in non-sexual physical ways. One way to cope with this cross-wiring and have sex anyway is to numb ourselves and depersonalize sex. This is often the case with prostitutes.

People who have dutiful sex are victims of an insidious kind of physically abusive relating. One cultural rule that people who are married or living together must have sex has resulted in countless numbers of people who are having sex when they don't want to. The effect is a violation of our sexuality as well as our spirit from the double damage of the intrusion into our bodies and the prohibition of conscious awareness of the violation.

Traumas And Addiction

Distresses from these traumas contribute to the cross-wiring of sexual energy and to our tendency to use sexual energy addictively. When we neither feel nor express our distresses, we use energy to repress them along with the traumas of childhood. As we keep more and more trauma out of consciousness, we create an imitation of life while suppressing real life feelings. Addictive behaviors are convenient for this because their purpose is to avoid real feelings. Alternatives to addiction are depression or other emotional symptoms.

5

Sex Isn't How We Thought It Would Be

Our culture, filtered through our parents and other adults and then through our adult selves and our partners, distorts sexual energy for each one of us. None of us escaped the influence of our culture, and none of us grew up fully able to know and use our sexual energy in enriching ways.

In this chapter I will address some of the cross-wired experiences you may be having. Cross-wiring can be as minor as needing to have sex in the same bedroom or as major as being able to achieve full arousal only when in pain. Both these cross-wirings, however, prohibit people from allowing their inner selves to tell them when and where and with whom to have sex. If we can only be aroused by people who are thin, of the opposite sex, the same age or blond, we are limited in our selection of a life partner by the programming created in childhood. Even more limiting are the need for sadomasochism and other specific sexual activities for arousal.

We are also limited in the capacity to *feel arousal emerging from the relationship* — instead, cross-wiring dictates what is arousing. As we relinquish cross-wiring, our natural arousal can emerge to replace it — an arousal that can be deeper, fuller and more satisfying than the intense drive or subdued interest resulting from childhood experiences. Cross-wiring makes it difficult to be aware of our partner, instead inviting fantasy or focusing on sexual arousal. When cross-wiring dominates, it becomes the center of sex and afterwards leaves us feeling empty and needing more of the same. The emptiness comes from participating in an illusion of intimacy — an illusion which ends with the ending of arousal.

Cross-wired sex can be a likely candidate for addiction because of its intensity and its illusionary nature. *Sex emerging from a real relationship where cross-wiring has been removed cannot be used addictively.* This is because addiction is designed to avoid the unpleasantness of reality. Healthy sexual energy, which can only be experienced in a nonaddictive state, is part of the positive reality that gets lost along with the unpleasant parts. This is why one approach to addressing our addictive use of sexual energy is to unwire the cross-wiring that made it likely for us to use our sexual energy addictively.

There are infinitely more possibilities. You can learn from your healing process something about the cross-wiring that took place while you were growing up and the resulting distortions of your sexual energy.

Sex Addiction

True addiction is characterized by compulsions that are out of control, threaten jobs and relationships, and make life unmanageable. The "drug trance," that crazed state that reduces our inhibitions and judgment, is so intense that it removes all sense of risk. We are dominated by the desire to act out sexually. Sexual energy has become the primary means of avoiding other feelings such as shame and loneliness. As we employ sexual energy in this way, it becomes impossible to experience the natural, inside-out purposes of sexuality.

Kenneth's drugged state began when he felt criticized or was in situations where he was expected to follow unclear rules. His mind would switch to thoughts of a woman looking adoringly at him and feeling drawn to his penis. This thought was enough to distract him from the terror elicited by criticism, but he had to keep it going. The next step to avoid his feelings was to think about buying pornographic magazines or seeing sexually explicit videos in "adult" book stores. The thoughts fed the trance until he was able to carry out his fantasies. The activities themselves increased the arousal. He didn't want to have an orgasm because he wanted the trance to continue for as long as possible. A favored activity that could go on for hours was driving in his car searching for a woman, sometimes a prostitute, while he fed the trance by looking at pictures in magazines. Often he would forget what he was searching for as the *feeling of searching* became addictive in itself.

When he had an orgasm or completed a sex act with a prostitute, sexual energy no longer numbed the feelings that seemed intolerable. Now the shame from his sexual activities and the compulsive spell he had been under added unwanted feelings. The addictive cycle was engaged, and he would begin again to stimulate himself into another addictive trance.

By anyone's definition Kenneth is a sex addict. I, on the other hand, did not look like an addict to the uninformed when I spent my high school days in fantasy about the mysterious man who would one day come and save me from emptiness and loneliness. Yet I also induced the addictive sexual trance with fantasy. It filled my body with non-genital sexual energy in such a way that I couldn't feel lonely.

James is also recovering from sex addiction. Driven by perfectionism, he found himself compulsively heading for sex video booths to escape feelings of impending failure. He was highly successful in his various professional roles, but never successful enough to quiet the fear that he would fail. Similar to James are most of the people who come to my classes and groups — they are successful in the world by our culture's definition of success. Yet inside many are torn apart by cultural and family admonitions to "succeed" and be what they are not.

Searching For Mr. Goodbar, a movie and book depicting the progressive nature of sexual addiction, portrays the story of a woman whose addiction results in compulsive, impersonal sex with drug use and finally death. In the beginning of the movie she engages in romantic fantasy, which fits within the norm of young womanhood. At that point she uses sexual energy addictively. She would not be diagnosed as a sexual addict until her compulsive behavior results in consequences such as difficulty making it to work on time.

The Addictive Use Of Sexual Energy

"The addictive use of sexual energy" is a broader term than "sexual addiction" which indicates that life is unmanageable because of sexual activity. The Continuum of Sexual Addictiveness in Chapter One shows what the differences are. Here are some examples:

1. If you find that sex and an orgasm provide relief from stress or tension, you are among the many who use *sex as a tranquilizer.* Our culture supports this use in the same way it supports social drinkers who use alcohol to unwind or to feel more comfortable when going to social gatherings. The person who drinks this way may not be an alcoholic, but the alcohol is used in the same way that an addict uses it — *to change feelings.*

The price for people who drink this way is that they don't get the opportunity to find out their real feelings and address them. The price is higher if we use sex this way. Not only does addictive use of sexual energy rob us of our feelings, but it also diminishes the possibility of finding out the real value of sex. Any addictive use of sexual energy leads us toward further addictive use, which is incompatible with the natural, unfolding, inside-out experience. We have to make a choice.

2. Alex was not a sex addict when I knew him, but it was apparent that he used sexual energy addictively because the need for *sexual reassurance* consumed a great deal of his energy in nonproductive ways. His mood was altered during the day, but not to the extent that he couldn't do well at his highly technical job. He felt agitated much of the time as he focused on whether his wife would have sex with him that night. He felt the need for reassurance of her love and believed that sexual attention provided it. For this reason his wife didn't want to have sex with him very often. Her disinclination, however, fueled his obsession.

3. *Infatuation* that goes beyond the early weeks of a new relationship is another common, culturally acceptable way of using sexual energy. My own experience with infatuation is that it distracted me from my real life, inhibited intimate relating with my friends and totally cut off my creativity. During one partic-

ularly intense period of infatuation (a natural successor to the romantic fantasy of my earlier years) I became aware of how disruptive it was and decided it was a symptom I wanted to examine. I could no longer delight in the sexualized, cocooned state that involved me and only one other person.

4. A very large percentage of people engage in *flirting* as a fun pastime. I had no interest in stopping this use of sexuality until I realized it was interfering with the wholesome relating I wanted. I had to see that when I introduced flirtatious energy into a group I *set up competition among the women and among the men,* furthering the schism between the sexes. I had to be willing to give up the feelings of power that came with flirting. It was also difficult because no one I associated with told me that what I was doing might be unhealthy. When I was ready to stop using sexual energy in this way, I had no mirrors for what I had been doing and no support for the changes.

The examples are endless. You can check out your own addictive uses of sexual energy by asking yourself the following questions when you find sexual energy coming up:

1. Is this sexual energy emerging gently out of my spiritual center?

Or is it grabbing me, stimulated from outside of myself?

2. Is the sexual arousal I feel three-dimensional, filling and flooding me, enhancing all my other feelings?

Or is it one-dimensional intensity that can prevent me from having other feelings?

3. Do I feel warmly relaxed, breathing easily and fully, as I welcome sexual arousal?

Or do I feel tensed up, muscles hard and tight, and breathing hard with arousal?

Learning to recognize our addictive use of sexual energy is a long process because we have so much support from our culture to maintain it. Working with others who are also examining their own and society's addictions can greatly speed up the process.

If You Don't Want Sex

The complete lack of interest in sexual feeling or activity can be just as serious a disturbance of sexual energy as addiction. Both are approaches to an energy that is confusing, contaminated and frightening. Addiction is an unconscious way to continue to feel like a sexual person. The unconscious decision not to be overtly sexual is another way to deal with the same distresses. If you don't feel sexual, you won't feel frightened. Our culture accepts this choice more easily for women, although both choices are made by both sexes.

It is also possible to make both choices at the same time. Elizabeth came to my Healthy Sexual Energy class to find out why she didn't want to have sex with her husband. During the exercises she learned she was using sexual energy addictively by carrying on a flirtatious, sexless affair. Her sexuality was given expression, but in a way that did not elicit her fear.

If you are choosing not to have sex, you are sacrificing a major part of being human, a part of you that can enhance connection with yourself, another person and the earth. It is an important symptom to examine as you reclaim healthy sexual energy. In my work with clients I have observed three areas to explore in learning why a person isn't interested in sex:

1. *Childhood experiences.* People who were victimized for an adult's sexual purposes may find that sex is too frightening to experience. The easiest choice seems to be to omit it from life. While this choice may have served you well as a young person buffeted about by the crazy dating world of our culture, it is no longer the only one. You can now go back into your childhood to remove the harsh effects of the treatment you received.

As you work toward reclaiming sexual comfort, it is essential that you have *complete control over your sexual activity*. The changes you make in your willingness to have sex must be only for you, not for your partner or to meet social requirements. You must be able to say *no* before you can say yes. When you were a child you couldn't say no. Now you can.

2. *Our culture.* We — men and women — have all been shamed for being sexual when we were growing up, and now we are forbidden to talk about it. We can avoid feelings of contamination and confusion by not being sexual.

3. *Our relationship.* Loss of sexual interest in a relationship commonly results when people hold in anger or other feelings or keep secrets. Alex's perception of sex as reassurance of love prevented his wife from engaging in an openly loving use of sex. She unconsciously knew he was misinterpreting her actions to mean she was loving him with sex, when actually he was searching for safety and reassurance through her willingness. But she

wasn't conscious of her reasons for refusing sex, so she felt guilty and unloving and went to therapy to find out why she was "frigid." While she also had issues stemming from her childhood and cultural expectations, the primary focus was identifying her perceptions of what was happening in the present. When she did, she could see why she did not want to have sex with Alex.

Having Unwanted Sex

Marriage and live-together relationships are defined in part by the fact that the couple has sex. An unspoken agreement is that we will meet the "sexual needs" of our partner as a part of the coupling contract. When one person doesn't want to have sex, either temporarily or permanently, it is cause for distress on the part of both. When this happens, many of us choose to have sex anyway.

Having sex when we don't want to distorts the use of sexual energy and will prevent us from knowing the inside-out, unfolding variety. If we violate ourself in order to live up to a cultural rule or to make sure our partner doesn't leave, then we are forcing sexual arousal to serve a lie. Healthy sexual energy can only be present when it is entirely right to be sexual.

Reducing The Fear Of Sex

The extensive shaming and consequent cross-wiring of sexual energy have created a population that is quite afraid of sex. You may be aware that you are afraid to have sex and you may have decided not to have sex to avoid that fear. Or you may be one of the many of us who use methods to arouse sexual interest to overcome the fear.

Many aids to overcoming the fear of sex have been devised, some the objects of a billion-dollar market and others based on the brain's creativity. They include pornography, alcohol and other drugs, using novelty to stimulate sexual interest, romance, lust and even telling jokes.

Pornography

Pornography is designed to reduce fear by stimulating sexual interest. Night clubs with nudity and sexual energy, "adult" book stores and video booths, books and magazines, etc., bring in vast amounts of money from millions of customers. If you use such methods to stimulate sexual interest, you are certainly not alone. Yet every man who has told me about his use of pornography has felt deep shame as if he were the only person doing this. One function of classes and groups that are focused on healthy sexual energy is to share secrets and find out that many other ordinary people have the same secret. Men, in particular, cannot admit to being afraid of sex or having difficulty becoming interested in sex because of the intense cultural prescriptions for being a "real man." One function of pornography is to assist men in living up to the cultural expectation of "always being ready."

Alcohol And Other Drugs

Drugs and alcohol serve to reduce fear and free people up to allow sexual arousal. The price is that the unconsciousness produced by the drug also renders the sex unconscious, and we become incapable of experiencing healthy sexual energy.

Novelty

Newness is always stimulating for humans, so new sex partners will create an outside-in interest that a long-term partner may not. Many people use this extra stimulation to override the fear of sex. The price is that a long-term, loving sexual relationship cannot develop because the fear re-emerges as the relationship ages. Women are socially permitted to couple and then to lose interest in sex. Men are required by our culture's rules to continue to be sexual and so have a harder time with committing to a relationship in which they no longer want sex. A man is also supported in believing it's his partner's fault because she doesn't seduce him or doesn't pay as much attention to him as she used to or has gained weight. If we have no fear of sex, these outside-in factors can have no importance because they are irrelevant to the inside-out unfolding of sexual energy that emerges from the relationship.

Having sex in new places and in new ways is often designed to override the disinclination to be sexual. Dr. Ruth Westheimer, the well-known TV sex therapist, encourages people to use these temporary methods to rekindle sexual arousal. She suggests other outside-in methods such as impersonal "quickies," sexual fantasy and deceiving our partner. This approach to sexuality can encourage the addictive use of sexual energy and prevents inside-out healing.

Fantasy

Sexual fantasy before and during sex is an easy way to move out of the present and distract oneself from the fear of sex. Cross-wired activities, either in fantasy or reality, will reproduce the sexual arousal that was present when they were first cross-wired.

Romance

Romance is a conversion of genital sexual feelings into a form that was acceptable to adults who shamed us in childhood. Romantic interaction can express sexual energy with no arousal felt in the genitals. Strong romantic feelings can actually make sex enjoyable for a woman who has no genital arousal. I experienced this for the first year I was having sex. I, the sexual fantasy addict, did not experience genital arousal, and yet having sex was intense and I was constantly drawn to it. Men have more difficulty with this use of romance because intercourse requires an erection, which is difficult to achieve without arousal.

Lust

Lust is another conversion of sexual feelings into a form intense enough to prevent fear. Lust focuses outside the self and makes use of cross-wiring and cultural conditioning to define what is sexually attractive. By feeding an outside-in arousal, lust prevents the fear of sex from emerging.

Telling Jokes

Joking is a common way to allow ourselves to break the rule that we mustn't talk about sex. References to sex by using sentences with two meanings and telling sex jokes are a way to bring sex into a conversation and discharge some of the stored-up sexual energy. It also creates an outside-in arousal. As with many fear reducers, sexual jokes can be used by sex addicts to create their drug.

People who are afraid of their sexual selves, sexual activities or sexual intimacy find that after they have completed sex the fear returns. This is often seen in "rolling over and going to sleep" immediately after sex. The partner usually interprets this to mean a lack of genuine caring, which it may be. It can also mean that reality is back and with it a need for distance.

Fear Of Intimacy

Intimacy can be defined as knowing and being known by another person. This knowing can be physical, sexual, intellectual and emotional — a spiritual connection. We all want intimate contact because it is one of our human potentials that contributes to a joyful and meaningful life. Sex is only one activity that provides the opportunity for intimacy, but it is a powerful one because it can open doors to a primitive, non-socialized experience of oneself and union with another. Through physical and emotional bonding sex can permit us to re-experience the merger of mother and infant, a life-giving time that is valuable for the developing child. In contrast to the ideal loving fusion, even mildly abusive backgrounds make the merger with another seem frightening. At the same time sex in a loving relationship offers the hope of allowing a safe, primitive merger of two people into one being. The choice to replace intimate sex with an outside-in, lustful or indifferent sexual arousal seems to make sense to a mind that doesn't want to reenact its particular childhood. Our culture supports this choice.

Philosophers have many theories to explain why the very thing we want most is frightening to us. This fear is one cause of addiction because addiction prevents intimacy. Impersonal sex with a stranger or a spouse can feel safer than intimate sex. Anne Wilson Schaef addresses this in her book *Escape From Intimacy*.

Sexual Arousal That We Do Not Choose

By asking us to repress our sexuality and then stimulating it, our culture has conditioned us to respond with sexual arousal to nudity, other people engaged with sexual energy and pictures of sexual poses. This conditioning, along with our particular cross-wiring, sets us up to have sexual feelings when we would not have chosen them. The massive cultural repression of natural sexual energy is accompanied by its eruption everywhere around us. The repression causes that energy to simmer just under the surface of experience. Stimuli associated with sexual arousal will easily trigger a reaction.

My own experience with sexual healing showed me it is possible to watch people have sex and not to have a sexual reaction. This is true with explicit movies and when watching people who are interacting sexually in public. I recently watched a couple "making love" while waiting for an order at a fast food restaurant in the very early morning. It was evident they had just emerged from bed and were going to return there with their food. They did not touch each other's genitals or kiss passionately, but they were as completely sexual as if they were in bed with no clothes on. It was quite beautiful to watch as their sexual energy encircled them. They touched each other gently, looking deeply into one another's eyes. The few people who entered the restaurant were clearly uncomfortable with the intense sexual energy and turned away from them. I was delighted to find that I had no unbidden erotic response, and instead could observe as if I were watching a ballet.

When we unwire our cross-wiring and examine and relinquish our culture's rules, it becomes possible to choose when we will be sexual and to be aroused only at those times.

Sex Doesn't Seem Loving

Sex can seem like too much work. It has to be done "right." Some people are having sex because they are supposed to. Some are not because they aren't supposed to. Fear of sex gets in the way. Anger expressed with sex can be damaging. Loving doesn't happen between two people when one or both imagine they are somewhere else. Unexpressed feelings can turn sex into an act. Many cross-wirings and cultural edicts prevent us from using sex to bond and re-bond lovingly.

Preferring Masturbation To Sex With A Partner

If you prefer to have sex by yourself, with or without pornography, you might take a look at your fears of intimacy or performance pressures. You might make this choice because relationships haven't worked out and it seems easier not to pursue that route. Another possibility is that sexual activities which seem necessary to arouse you aren't acceptable to your partner or to yourself and you feel stuck with your cross-wiring. Without an understanding of cross-wiring and how to unwire it you have had no choice.

Masturbation is one way to make love to oneself. However, if it is the only way we can express sexual energy then something got cross-wired and is preventing us from bonding to a partner with sexual energy.

By the time he reached his limit of conflict and heartache in his mid-30s, Robert had had a series of relationships, including several years of marriage. When his last relationship ended because his lover complained of his inability to maintain erections, he sighed a huge sigh of relief and focused on his life alone. He created a home that was his own and put energy into his work and friendships. Any indication that a woman was interested in him was pleasantly received, but not furthered. As months turned into years, he developed a sex life with himself that seemed satisfying. He took good care of his body, working out and eating a healthy diet. He made love to himself — attending to each part of his body, not focusing on his genitals. Almost every evening he set aside time to bathe, possibly read and then bring himself to orgasm before going to sleep.

The choice Robert made is one that works quite well for many people, particularly when knowledge about causes of cross-wiring and methods for unwiring it are not available. When I knew Robert I did not understand these connections and so could not offer them to him. I am now aware, as I look back on stories he told, that he was sexually abused by his mother in the form of flirtatious attention to him as her little lover. He didn't trust women once they indicated a sexual interest in him.

Flirting Creates Illusion And Violates Boundaries

Flirting is a drug. It introduces outside-in sexual energy for the purpose of creating false relationship intensity and to increase feelings of outside-in self-esteem. We are valued for being "sexy," and we can get intense attention from others by flirting. Why would we stop?

Flirting is a shortcut that has a number of negative consequences. Real friendship becomes short-circuited and cannot develop well. The exclusive nature of sexualized relating evokes jealousy of partners or others present. Feelings of outside-in self-esteem derived from flirting are temporary. Instead of making us more connected to people, which is the intent, even successful flirting makes us more lonely. The connection with another person is only an illusion.

Flirting is an addictive use of sexual energy because it creates something that doesn't emerge from the real nature of the relationship and distracts us from the real relationship. If you want to reclaim your healthy sexual energy, examining your use of flirting is one route to finding out about your cross-wiring. As you unwire it, you will find that your interest in flirting will decrease.

In our sexualized society, natural sexual boundaries are difficult to identify. We all know intuitively when ours have been violated, but the voice that tells us seems soft compared to the voices of our culture that say anything is fine between consenting adults. We are urged to consent to the flirting of those around us. If you are a man you are considered less than masculine if you don't respond to flirtation or notice the body in clothes worn to get your attention. Women are allowed to object angrily, but only if flirting goes to the point of sexual harassment. When we have the courage to respond to those soft voices that let us know when sexual energy interferes with whole, human relating, then they will become louder and more audible.

I believe one of the reasons flirting has become part of our typical social behavior is because of the many sex addicts in our society who are not identified as such. We are encouraged to go along with the flirtation of addicts, most of whom are constantly aware of sexuality and want to interact sexually on any level. Many addicts lace their conversations with sexual material and bring sexual awareness to those around them by their facial expressions and posturing. As sex addicts push the limits of the acceptable, their targets have been unable to intuitively know appropriate limits and have actually changed their beliefs in accordance with the addict's rationalizations. As all of us use sexual energy addictively, we become unable to know when someone else is introducing inappropriate sexual interaction. "Date rape" is one result of this naivete. Another is men having sex when they really don't want to because they are responding to the rule of masculinity that they can't refuse sex.

Kenneth described to me a scene in which a woman he had met only hours before in a class "came on" to him. She did this by posturing sexually and touching his sides with small strokes. When he was actively in his addiction he valued such approaches, even though he was in a relationship. He had no awareness, until he experienced loving sexual energy, that she was violating his boundaries by sexualizing and crossing over the line of personal physical contact with a stranger.

Using Seduction

One of our cultural beliefs is that we have a sex drive and it makes us want sex. Some people have a stronger drive and want sex more than those with a weaker drive. This is a fallacy that stems from our inability to grow up with healthy sexual energy. The belief in a sex drive results in the notion that each of us wants sex at a rate that our body determines and that has little to do with our relationship. If a person's time has arrived, then he or she goes to the partner or goes out to find a partner and initiates sexual contact. The partner then responds by having sex or indicating that he or she is not interested. When finding a partner becomes difficult, those with the "higher sex drives" must learn the art of seduction. Single and coupled people alike learn seduction games.

In contrast, if sex is an unfolding of energy for the purpose of bonding, or creating a spiritual connection to a partner and our essential selves, then one person would not be trying to seduce another person into it. The energy to unite comes from both at the same time or not at all. We are fully capable of having no sexual interaction for months or years, as we are capable of having several sexual interactions in a day. The frequency is determined by the need to use sexual energy. This is why the frequency of sex is higher in the early, bonding period of a relationship and then becomes sporadic when the bonding is complete. Sex is then valuable for a loving expression of the relationship or for re-bonding after each person has been involved with some other area of his or her life for a time.

Telling Your Childhood Story Of Sexual Abuse Through Pornography

The use of pornography is distressing to many who use it and brings people to my classes on healthy sexual energy. While women use pornography, most of it is designed for men — the primary market for the billion-dollar business. Men come to my classes with the hope of ridding themselves of a curse, and women come to find out about their man's use of it.

Pornography elicits sexual arousal from the outside in. It employs the cross-wiring from our childhood sexual abuse situations and from our culture's prescriptions to create stimuli that will trigger sexual arousal. For example, Kenneth found he was aroused by the sight of a large penis being put into a woman's mouth. He went to pornographic video stores or looked at pictures and scanned for this scene. Other scenes had no effect on his addictive arousal. After we began to uncover his memories of childhood sexual abuse, he discovered that his father had put his penis down Kenneth's throat repeatedly until he was about three years old. Kenneth learned to stop his gag reflex voluntarily to accommodate the penis. As a teen he "swallowed" knives, having "forgotten" why he became able to not gag.

This is a dramatic example of the connection between abuse as a child and adult choice of pornography. All of us have such connections, and we can find out what they are by observing our reactions to different kinds of stimuli. I experienced this when I went to an American Psychological Association convention several years ago and attended a workshop on pornography. I walked into a theater that was playing a documentary of various kinds of pornography and sat down to an odd experience. As the film changed from one kind of stimulation to another, I found my sexual arousal coming up and then dropping, to come up again as the scene matched my cross-wiring. The biggest surprise was finding that I could watch some of the actors having

intercourse and not become aroused even though having intercourse arouses me. This was the beginning of my understanding
that we aren't automatically aroused by sexual activities. It isn't
part of our human heritage to find our sexual energy coming up
when we are watching or hearing other people engage sexually.
These reactions are a result of cross-wiring of sexual energy
that are unavoidable when growing up in our culture.

We are all mishandled and our sexual boundaries not respected, which results in our sexual energy being aroused from the
outside of us. This outside-in sexual arousal becomes associated
with different things — the body part that is stimulated, the
kind of handling, the kind of person doing the handling, etc.
When we reach adulthood, our culture affirms that arousal
from cross-wiring is actually very good and helps us to get
more of it. Some well-known sex therapists help people to produce more cross-wired arousal.

Sexual energy that is elicited by cross-wiring feels driven, in
contrast to the loving use of sexual energy that emerges and
unfolds from inside of us. While the former seems to be an
intense, pleasurable state, it prevents us from knowing ourself
(and our partner, if we are with someone else). As long as we
believe this kind of arousal is the real nature of sexuality, then
we are prevented from finding out about the other variety —
the kind that expands and grows as the personal connection
grows, and that diminishes when anything interferes with that
connection (with ourself or with another).

Some feminist writers differentiate between "pornography"
and "erotica," seeing the former as bad because it objectifies
and oppresses women and the second as acceptable sexually
stimulating material. In the pursuit of healthy sexual energy,
both will inhibit the evolution of natural, wholesome, life enriching sexuality.

People use pornography for many reasons. One is to avoid
the fear of sex, as discussed earlier. A second reason is that it
permits a person to be sexual without intimacy or bonding,
whether the sex is alone or with another person. In our boun-
daryless society many of us grew up with constant violations of
our physical and emotional boundaries, and so we prefer to live
a life of separateness. We can put up strong shields to ward off
the penetration of another's wants and stay safe from further
violation. Those who grow up this way do not have models of
how to comfortably set limits and create boundaries, so the

alternative seems to be a strong shield. When we are sexual, the shield is in danger of slipping because the physical intimacy of sex invites us to drop our shields — one of its wonderful functions. The use of pornography, including its fantasy version, allows one to be sexual and remain safe.

I worked with a man I'll call Bret who wanted to be a loner although he was quite sociable. His wife didn't want to have sex after the initial period of bonding, and they came to me for this and other difficulties. As we examined Bret's sexual relating, he told me that he always fantasized when he was having sex and didn't want his wife to talk so he wouldn't be distracted from his thoughts. He also preferred a darkened room. I recommended that he stop himself when he began to fantasize and see what happened. At first he couldn't create enough arousal to have intercourse, but in time he found other information appearing. He had to see that the woman he was in bed with was his wife, and that he had feelings toward her he had not expressed. He felt pressured by her preference for a state of constant closeness, and he allowed her needs to violate his boundaries. The only way he could be sexual with her was to have his shield in place, which was brought about by fantasy. This information allowed him to work on his need to know his boundaries and make them clear to her. He began to use his desire for fantasy as information that he wasn't taking care of his needs.

Our choice of pornography can also be a way of telling our childhood story. Our unconscious minds are always trying to find means to bring into public those childhood abuses that we were not allowed to fully remember and experience. The commandment "Thou Shalt Not Be Aware" works most effectively with childhood sexual experiences. However, they continue to fight for expression in adult years. Pornography and other sexual services are one opportunity to express our response to childhood sexual abuses. Once we tell our story, this need for pornography can decrease.

My experience at the pornography workshop gave me information to use to reclaim my healthy sexual energy. For example, I saw that bondage scenes that weren't even very sexual aroused me, while penile penetration of vaginas didn't. As I reclaimed memories of the sexual abuse in my early childhood, being restrained while used for sexual purposes was a significant part of my experience. I wasn't vaginally penetrated so no crosswiring with my vagina occurred. While I enjoy lengthy intercourse as a delightful way to arouse sexual energy, I don't receive outside-in stimulation from watching it.

Pornography preferences can also be cross-wired from childhood experiences that do not include overt sexual acts. The shaming of sexuality that all of us experience can be crosswired to humiliation in sexual activities. We can take the position we held as a child and be aroused by being humiliated, or we can take the position of the one who shamed us and become aroused by humiliating another person. Humiliation can also prevent us from becoming aroused at all.

Our fantasies and our choices of pornography can provide useful information about damaging childhood experiences that we can use to heal ourselves. Assume it isn't an accident that certain things attract you. Then ask yourself questions about where the connection between sexual energy and these particular stimuli came from. The answers may not come right away because you have been well trained to Not Be Aware. If you keep asking, you will find out why you cannot be aware and eventually what created the connections.

Limiting Our Choices For A Sex Partner

One of our major tasks as we reach adulthood is to find a life partner with whom we will live, share a lifestyle and probably raise children. If we were to take on this task openly, we would see that we have the whole world to choose from — people of both sexes, all ages and all socioeconomic levels who are not yet partnered with someone else. But our cross-wiring greatly limits our choices. There is a myth that few people can qualify as our potential sex partner. While there is some logic in partnering with someone around the same age and with similiar lifestyle, these choices are not made from logic. We respond to strong prohibitions.

Our cross-wiring interacts with cultural prescriptions to limit our choices even further. Most people find thin people more attractive than fat ones and large breasts on women more valuable than small. Men with money and power actually look more physically attractive to many women than those who are poor.

6

Our Bodies:
The Vessels We
Live In

When we were little children, we loved being in our bodies. We didn't evaluate them as good or bad, we just lived. We touched and felt everywhere, exploring our vessel, and loved the feeling of our own touch. If the shame of the adults who attended us had not contaminated our sexual energy, we would have grown up with these same attitudes. We would not compete and compare. We might still base our evaluation of bodies on how functional they are and the effort we've put forth to improve them.

When I am physically fit and eating healthy food, my body feels wonderful to be in. When I eat poorly and don't exercise, I become sluggish and don't feel attractive. Our tissue changes as our feelings change. Depressed people have dense, opaque tissue that keeps the observer at a distance. Healthy, vibrant people have skin that seems almost translucent because the person inside is visible.

Altering posture to deal with emotional stresses can deform the body and make it unattractive. I had large pads of fat on my upper thighs that were only tolerable to me when I was very thin. Rolfing, which restructures the body, changed the position of my pelvis. This changed my hip joint and consequently the pads disappeared. My body took on the shape it was supposed to have naturally.

I learned later, during my work on childhood incest, that I had changed the position of my pelvis to protect it from abusive contact. I had what is called a posterior pelvis — I had tilted the top of my pelvis back and the bottom of it forward, resulting in flat buttocks with no lower back curve. This was in response to sexual touch from behind me. I was unconsciously trying to hide the part of my body that was the focus of the abuse. The fat on my outer thighs was a consequence of the postural change. I also had deposits of fat all around my upper thighs, which went away when I completed emotional work on the incest. They just melted away.

An anterior pelvis can also be a result of sexual abuse from the front of the body, and the sway back can result from the attempt to remove the genitals from touch. Stooped shoulders may reflect women's discomfort with breasts. Odd walks result from tight, stiff pelvises that become rigid from body memories stored there. Rolfing loosens up the fascia, the body packing material that is the medium used to create these changes. Rolfing removes the effects, and at the same time makes the related feelings more available.

Violating the natural positioning of the body makes it unattractive regardless of our cultural rules. When we are in touch with our bodies we can tell when something is "off" and what to do to correct it.

All of us have to work to become comfortable with our bodies because as we grow up we are shamed for a number of physiological functions. One of these is our sexuality. Others have to do with the elimination of urine and feces and the places from which they are eliminated. If we hadn't been shamed we would still be delighted with our genitals and our anuses.

To maintain our innate respect for our bodies, we need adults to respect them as well. In our culture children's bodies are considered their parents' property. Few parents know how to respect their children's right to control their own bodies (because each parent has not been given such respect). Parents confuse taking care of a child's body with controlling it. Even in those homes where parents have no inclination to hit their children or handle them roughly, it is clear to the children that the adult gets to decide what will happen. The child has no veto power.

An outcome of children's knowing that adults control their bodies is the current need to train children about what is sexually inappropriate to prevent sexual abuse. The irony is that *children already know what is abusive.* We are born knowing when we are being handled for the needs of someone else and when we are seen as objects instead of people with our own needs. Our culture does not mirror this inherent right back to the child. The child overrides intuitive knowledge and allows abuse.

Anna's mother asks her why she couldn't have just said no to her father when he was sexual with her. It was for the same reason he, as a respectable citizen and professional, could see fit to use her very young body for sexual gratification. He was socialized to believe that parents own their children and also that children don't remember and aren't affected by events in their very early years. And he had very poor sexual boundaries, also a product of his acculturation. Anna gathered this information from him by his actions and was well aware that she truly had no choice.

We enter our teen years already feeling bad about our bodies. Then increased sexual energy and body changes add to the confusion. As we adapt to these natural occurrences, we confront a culture with its ready-made criteria for physical acceptability which even specify body shape and face. These criteria are particularly cruel during teen years, setting in place further physical and sexual abuse. It is during these years that our peers place us on the EMPA (Externally Measured Physical Attractiveness) scale. That influences our outside-in self-esteem and further limits our selection of life partners to those who are at a similar place on the scale. A "good looking" man who is a "ten" cannot date a woman who is a "five" and certainly not a "one."

After my divorce I was in a brief relationship with a man who had been at the top of the EMPA scale when he was in high school. He had been good looking, a top athlete and gregarious. (He was also depressed, but that didn't affect the rating process.) After two marriages to very beautiful women, he knew he had to change the association of his worth with the looks of his mate or he would fail in relationships again. We discussed this with seriousness because I was older than he was and had never been a "ten" on the EMPA scale — both of which had made me off limits for him in the past. Even with his increased consciousness he could not stop evaluating *his* worth based on *my* physical attributes. He told me I was "attractive enough," but he could not delight in me physically because of his cross-wiring. The relationship, of course, could not continue.

Effects Of Body Shaming

A number of common views reflect the body shaming we receive throughout our lives. One is the desire most of us have to change our looks. Plastic surgery is used to reshape noses, remove fat deposits, raise and enlarge breasts, remove "extra" skin and otherwise change our looks to match more closely the cultural standard. Health spas advertise that their purposes are to improve health and attractiveness. They implicitly promise that clients will rate higher on the EMPA scale, even though the inherent attractiveness that comes with increased physical vitality is also an outcome of regular exercise and healthy diet.

Aging is a painful process in our culture because we become less and less attractive (and so less valuable) under the classic criteria. The cross-wiring that comes from these criteria must be unwired in order for us to feel more and more beautiful as the years pass. New criteria can replace the old ones: comfort in our body, increasing body awareness, increasing agility, increasing health and increasing ability to love with our body are some examples. We can also move to the place where no criteria apply — we just are!

A devastating effect of body shaming is the resulting lack of ability to listen to and understand our bodies. Most of us live in them as if we are merely visiting briefly; we don't move in for the long run, nest there and really get acquainted. Settling in is a requirement for learning about our sexual energy because sexual energy is physical and our body is its container. Thinking can be done entirely outside of the body with no awareness of our physical selves. This is why so many of us choose to be intellectual people — the intellect is less likely than the body to be shamed.

Yet as soon as we respond to shaming by no longer being aware of our bodies, we abandon the ability to sense what is going on in our body and what it needs. The results are many.

We have to be sick before knowing we need rest. We eat things that seem to taste good but we can't hear our body's objections. We feel really good when beginning an exercise program, but are accustomed to inertia setting in after a few weeks or months as the need to be physically dead outweighs the desire to feel alive. Good physical exercise makes us *feel*. In years past I prescribed exercise to depressed clients, knowing it would make them feel better. When absolutely *no one* took my advice, I began to figure out that the need to be depressed and immobilized was of foremost importance, and exercise would not allow that to continue. When the work on the causes of the depression is underway and people have experienced changes, then they are more able to engage in activity that permits them to experience themselves.

Healing our sexual energy means we get to appreciate our bodies. As we shed the outside-in evaluation, we can really examine ourselves and find our strengths and abilities — what our bodies truly can do. We can evaluate what we think is wrong with our bodies from a *functional* point of view, and then explore the many avenues to correcting it. Many people have gone before us in this quest. As a result there are several powerful forms of body work available. Yoga has been around for centuries, and with Tai Chi, is available to help us learn from the inside-out how to listen to our body and help it unfold. We can become familiar with the vessel we reside in, becoming aware of the messages it sends to us constantly about what it needs and what changes we might make to help it contain us more comfortably.

Chapter 14 will detail some ways you can become aware of your body again. Awareness is necessary to experience your sexual energy fully and to remove blocks that inhibit this energy from flowing freely through you.

7

Recognizing Our
Coupling Difficulties

Our sexual functioning encompasses three areas of our lives: our personal sexual history, the influences of our culture and the dynamics in our relationship. Relationships are a confusing area of relating for most people, as attested to by many books on the subject. Sexuality is influenced by issues that simmer under the surface and which we may not know how to address. This chapter will look at five of these issues.

Inability To Talk

The rule that we can't talk about sex prevents us from learning how to explore what is happening when sex doesn't feel right.

I have observed what happens when people receive permission to talk. I teach a four-week class called "Healthy Sexual

Energy and How to Reclaim It." Everyone has permission not to talk at all, so the class is less threatening than group therapy. Everyone is invited to talk, and exercises are done in which people can talk to each other in groups of three. There is a lot of fear the first couple of weeks, and then people begin to believe they really can violate the no-talking rule. By the last night the room is alive with energy as most people share something of their sexual experience that is really important to them. The other significant event is that most people become able to articulate the problem they are working on — it is no longer vague, undefinable and nameless.

The ways to start talking are described in later chapters on healing. Chapters 11 and 12 have instructions for couples on how to become conscious of barriers to sexual relating. The partners can use the relationship as a place for healing their *selves*, their *relationship* and their *sexuality*. (I recommend an excellent book by Harville Hendrix called *Getting the Love You Want*. He describes the influence of our history on our present relating and has useful exercises and methods for reclaiming ourselves.)

Lying To Protect Our Partner

The "don't-talk" rule is followed closely by the "lie-to-protect-them" rule. While we all aspire to honesty, at the same time we have a conflicting cultural requirement to withhold the truth if it would be painful to the other person or to ourselves. This rule is the cause of a great deal of misunderstanding and grief in relationships and prevents the unfolding of the loving use of sexual energy.

Bette was married for 15 years before she found out she was lying to her husband. Even though she was a therapist and had received extensive therapy, she fully accepted the cultural beliefs that we must not tell painful truths and that other people don't know when we are deceiving them. In addition, the "Thou Shalt Not Be Aware" rule made it difficult for her to even know she was lying to him.

She said she enjoyed sex with Harold, that there was something wrong with her because she didn't want to have sex very often and that she was in therapy to fix it. She believed this was true. She didn't tell him she pushed herself to have sex every five days or so to meet the marriage requirement. She didn't let him know she drank wine and masturbated in the bathtub while preparing for sex so she could get aroused enough to have the mandatory orgasm that demonstrated to him she had been satisfied.

Her husband also unknowingly lied. He told her that he wanted to please her with sex and that he really loved her. He didn't consciously know he was reenacting his relationship with his mother by being very good to her so she would give him loving attention. He didn't know that he wasn't using sex to love her, but instead was seeking reassurance.

Bette finally reached the point where she was ready to confront the situation. As she and Harold broke the rules and became able to talk openly about their marriage, both could see that they already knew the truths but had been unable to speak them. They learned they were living a lie that prevented them from reclaiming their loving. Once they gave themselves permission to talk about it, the floodgates opened. They talked for hours and even gave up TV for months because, after 15 years of silence, this new conversation fascinated them.

Bette had a hard time accepting that her disinclination to have sex with her husband was because of something covert on his part. She assumed that what was going on with her alone brought about a reluctance to do something she *"should"* want to do. Once she became aware that she was responding to something in him, she could make a conscious choice not to have sex to satisfy his patterned needs. When she had sex to reduce his fears, she wasn't being loved and the adult man she married wasn't receiving the loving she was giving.

Once they could talk about this, they were able to identify the issues and to be sexual only when they were two adults loving each other. The barrier was broken by seeing the truth and speaking it to each other.

Infrequent Sex

Another couple I saw in therapy were not having sex very often, and Donna described the problem as her husband's use of pornography. She wanted him to stop and wanted me to tell him it was wrong. She was too angry to have sex with him, particularly since she viewed the women in the pictures as rivals. Feeling guilty about the pornography, among other things, Steve also didn't want to have sex. The only way he could be sexual with Donna was to create a fantasy about another woman in a different place to distract him from the guilt. He didn't find this very enjoyable, but did it when he felt he should have sex.

Therapy revealed the fear he had of sex and the causes from his childhood. His mother had smothered him with "loving," not of a sexual nature but intrusive of his boundaries and oblivious to his needs. Any prolonged physical contact in which he felt his boundaries slipping away made him so uncomfortable that he felt an urgent need to escape. He had projected his childhood onto his present life with his wife.

Once Steve and Donna were aware of these dynamics, they had hope for working on them. Donna could begin to see that she wasn't being rejected or betrayed by his use of pornography, that it was a symptom of the abuse of Steve's childhood boundaries. Her anger diminished to concern and permitted her to work with Steve to remove the barrier between them. I taught them techniques to focus on the feelings that prevented them from using sex lovingly. This opened up doors to retrieve information so Steve could heal from his childhood.

In the case of Steve and Donna, one person's dynamics influenced the sexual relating, and yet it seemed to be the other's reactions that were the cause of the relationship's difficulties. Once they could talk to each other, the picture changed.

Unexpressed Or Misdirected Anger

If our partner suggests having sex when he or she is feeling angry toward us, and we are feeling uncomfortable about it, our reluctance has little to do with our past or our culture. There is an issue within the relationship that isn't apparent and that doesn't belong in the sexual arena. To use sex to express or mask anger is not a loving unfolding of sexual energy.

Withheld anger is a common reason for disturbance of sexual relating. It can manifest in a loss of interest in sex or in using sex to express anger indirectly. Rape is the most extreme form of anger that is expressed with sexual energy. There are a variety of milder forms, including pressuring our partner to have sex when it is apparent he or she doesn't want to. We can communicate pressure with no words. If we can know when we are angry and express it directly, then we won't contaminate sexual relating.

Over-attachment

Over-attachment to partners is a source of struggle that usually shows up in the sexual relationship. Marriage may seem essential to life, and many of us will make any sacrifice to maintain it. Such attachments are usually addictive. (Read Anne Wilson Schaef's book *Escape from Intimacy* for a more detailed account.) Addiction to "falling in love" or infatuation creates difficulties if a relationship becomes long-term.

Mark was addicted to the very sexual, romantic period of early love in which his lover expressed great interest in being with him. When this phase passed and the lover was ready to focus again on her own life, he would feel abandoned and end the relationship. When he became aware of his addiction, he could begin his recovery by examining the feelings of abandonment. Over time he came to see that relationships consist of alternating closeness and separateness. He could then relinquish the need for constant attention.

8

Tasks Of
Healing Ourselves

Developing Self-Compassion
And The Power Of Observation

Our society has transmitted a value to us about who is to "blame" for anything wrong. In business, government, car accidents, etc., it is necessary to find out who should have done something differently. The chosen person, group or country then has to pay in some way, either monetarily or with shame and apology. This kind of structure says we are to blame for our sexual behaviors and something is wrong with us for expressing them.

An even more devastating acculturated belief is that somehow we brought on the abusive experiences in our childhood that shaped our cross-wiring. This belief is a great obstacle to finding out what happened and how it affected us.

If we carry this belief, we must also carry the responsibility for changing or not changing it and the shame that comes with doing things that are socially unacceptable. This is damaging because shame will only serve to inhibit us from learning what we need to know. A helpful book for people recovering from sexual damage is *Healing the Shame that Binds You*, by John Bradshaw.

Here are some important things to remember as you begin healing:

- You are entirely deserving of compassion for yourself.
- You didn't cause your cross-wiring.
- You cannot control the sexual choices that are not working well for you.
- You want to find your true sexual energy and use it well.
- You have not had people around you who could help you with this process; instead, you are surrounded by people who also believe it is your fault and all you have to do is really want to change.
- You deserve an accurate mirror.

Compassion for yourself and knowledge of the role your past and your culture have played in your choices are necessary before you can feel safe enough to plunge into this painful work. The shame that was put on you when you were young can arise as you look at yourself. If you shame yourself for everything you learn, then it becomes difficult to continue learning. (Some people's shaming runs so deep that they will shame themselves for shaming themselves.)

As your shame diminishes, you will be able to observe what is taking place. Once you are able to observe what you are feeling, thinking and doing without shame, you will automatically change in ways that benefit your loving nature. When we are free to learn we will do so automatically. It is built into our human nature.

Learn To Talk

Sex is universally off limits for open discussion. One result is that we aren't able to undo the damage that occurs in our childhood or to challenge our culture's dealings with sexuality. *Even the sexual revolution of the 60s, which brought about a major shift in the way people engaged sexually, did not change the discomfort over discussing sex openly and comfortably.*

The first time I ask a class to divide up and talk to two other people about a detail of their sex life, the room immediately changes. Unspoken feelings flow and walls go up. The ambience of the room is dramatically different. I gave a workshop on talking about sex to psychologists who had clients dealing with incest issues, and the reaction was the same. When they divided into groups of three and talked, the room was filled with low, confidential voices.

Learning to talk about sex is essential to making changes. This is more easily done in a class or groups that are formed for this purpose. As people become comfortable, talking with friends can assist liberation from the "no-talk" rule.

When I am talking with people I don't know well and who are not yet comfortable talking about sex, I begin by speaking only theoretically. I might talk about the "no-talk" rule or the shaming of sexuality that we all have had. I watch to see how the person reacts, and if he or she is defensive and uncomfortable I stay at this level. If the person responds with interest and shares her or his own experience, then I move to a more personal level. This way I can check out the safety of sharing *before* I talk about things I don't want someone to put down. This testing of the water allows me to find people who are able to continue opening up with me and who allow me to open up with them. There is nothing to be gained from talking to people who will re-shame you because that reinforces your childhood experience instead of contradicting it.

Chapter 11 goes into detail about how to tell your story and Chapter 13 outlines a plan for creating a support group as you get underway with learning how to talk about sex.

Develop Your "Sniffer"

We live in a culture that provides very little truth about sexual energy. We who teach are still limited by our culture and do not have "the answers." Even if we did, accepting a new ruling to replace our culture's old ones will leave us still outside ourselves following rules. The alternative is to develop our own awareness from the inside-out about what is right for us.

A way to do this is to don an anthropologist's hat as if we are from another culture or planet and have come to study the odd way people here attempt to relate to each other. This kind of study, of course, is much easier when we don't belong to the culture because we wouldn't have internalized its rules — including the commandment Thou Shalt Not Be Aware. We have to go through an education process that includes examining our own inhibitions against knowing as well as the rulings of our culture.

Rex and I invented the term "sniffer" to mean the intuitive part of us that knows when behaviors, thoughts and feelings are synchronized with a larger whole. We will make a sniffing sound to indicate we are assessing whether something seems "off." For example, when I see a woman looking at Rex in a flirtatious way I might make a sniffing sound to communicate my observation to him. This alerts him to examine what is happening if he hadn't seen it already. We also sniff at each other when we suspect the other one is engaging in a pattern from childhood. The information is useful so we can examine what we are doing and change it.

With our sniffers on we "sniff" through the data all around us, which includes our feelings, other people's feelings, cultural rules and the attempts of others to control us when we are onto truths that are uncomfortable for them. As our sniffers become clear we spot these things more and more quickly and then have the freedom to make different choices — from the inside out.

Kathryn's story is a good example of how we can become anthropologists in our own culture. After some months of therapy she decided my views were superior to those she learned in her childhood, so she adopted them. At the same time she was developing a good sniffer but had difficulty believing her own sniffer could be right after 30 years of being told by our culture and her mother that her views were wrong.

Kathryn came to a session with puzzlement over something I had said months before about protecting a new relationship by limiting contact with old lovers and keeping clear on communication to avoid misunderstandings. New relationships, I told her, are fraught with fears from childhood which are easily triggered in that early love state. My statement had become dogma for her and for her lover, who quoted it back to her when she did things that were uncomfortable for him. She was feeling controlled, and her sniffer didn't agree that it was inappropriate to develop friendships with other men. However, she also felt constrained to obey the statements of her teacher — me.

As we talked she could see that adopting something I said from the outside-in didn't work, and that she had to obey her sniffer instead. My statement, while valuable in context, could not be generalized and interpreted to fit all other situations. Its real value to her was as a suggestion of a new way to look at love relationships that she could take inside, sniff over and keep as a backdrop for further experiences. The general idea, "protect a new love relationship," would then become hers to be employed as her sniffer deemed best. Kathryn's developing respect for her sniffer allowed her to let go of my statement and make decisions regarding her relationship that felt right for her.

This book is filled with ideas that you can use to inform your sniffer so it can sniff more clearly. The ideas will lose their usefulness if they are adopted outside-in. If you use them inside-out, they can expand inside you to become far more than I could imagine.

Healing Our Addictive Use Of Sex

Our addictive use of sex can decrease as our physical, emotional and social consciousness raises. As we become aware of how we use addictions to avoid reality, and as we address the reality we wanted to avoid, we have less and less need to act addictively. We all have in us a desire to live fully and richly which will take over as we give it freedom.

Becoming conscious requires experiencing the pain of those feelings we are avoiding. With the support of other recovering people we can feel the shame and loneliness that underlie addictive uses of sexual energy, and we can examine and relinquish them. Chapter 9 addresses ways to work with compulsive behaviors and obsessions in the early stages of recovery. As you become acquainted with their function and the cross-wiring that created the form of our addictions, you will be ready to engage in the long-term, unfolding work of healing.

Unwiring Our Cross-Wiring

Identifying our cross-wiring provides information we can use to heal from the misuse of our sexual energy. Cross-wiring comes from our childhood experiences, our culture's bizarre rules and myths and our adult love relationships, as I have described in previous chapters.

The anthropologist's hat you use to educate your cultural-rule sniffer is also useful for identifying your cross-wiring. The task is to educate your sniffer so it alerts you when something is going on that isn't pure inside-out sexuality. The following can help you open doors to the childhood and cultural experiences that wired your sexuality in ways that interfere with inside-out, unfolding of sexual bonding. As you study the data you obtain, sharing it with other healing people can elicit their support. This is some of the hard work of recovery because feelings of shame will come up as you examine the evidence of your cross-wiring. Keep breathing and let the shame flow through you and out. Talking to others will keep the shame at a lower level.

What Goes On In Your Fantasy Life?

All of us have sexual fantasies. Fantasies are thoughts about sex we have had, sex we will have or sexual activities we wouldn't choose to engage in but that arouse sexual feelings. They also include fantasies of romantic love that are propelled by sexual energy, even if no overt sexual activities occur.

What Kind Of Pornography Arouses You?

Video booths in "adult" book stores give evidence of the wide variety of cross-wiring. Each booth has a large selection of videos and customers can flip through the channels to find the ones that represent their cross-wiring.

- Kenneth watched only those videos that showed a very large penis being put into a woman's mouth and down her throat. As a young child he had his father's penis shoved down his throat, cutting off his breathing.
- Rick went to booths for the "human" contact of his mouth on another man's penis. His father had "allowed" him to suck on his penis when he was a child.
- Bob wasn't aroused by watching videos. Stimulation required the excitement of having a woman look at him with sexual desire.

- An example of my cross-wiring was finding myself aroused by the arousal of the people in the video, regardless of their activities. Each person's cross-wiring results in different needs to produce outside-in sexual arousal.

What Kinds Of Activities Are Sexually Arousing To You?

I have described Anna's need for anal stimulation to create an intense outside-in arousal and orgasm. When she unwired this, she still found anal stimulation pleasurable but she no longer experienced it as necessary. Once her natural arousal was available, she didn't have to do something to force arousal.

Kenneth was aroused by watching penises go in mouths, including his own penis in the mouths of his lovers. His childhood experience of having his father's penis pushed down his throat cross-wired this activity with arousal. Intercourse held little appeal until he was able to reclaim his healthy sexual energy.

These are examples of obvious cross-wiring. Many of our preferences are socially sanctioned and so more difficult to detect. Examples are: preference for the man on top during intercourse, preference for sexual activities directed by the man, focus on the woman's responsiveness, the need for orgasm to follow intercourse and the need for orgasm to end sex. The list is endless. These forms of cross-wiring are harder to identify as harmful to inside-out sexual unfolding and so are more difficult to change. The anthropologist in you will have to abandon the idea that there are right ways to have sex. Then you can explore, allowing cross-wirings to come to your consciousness one at a time.

As cross-wirings reach consciousness they become doors into the past and to our culture so you can become aware of traumas you have experienced. You can then re-experience these traumas, release them by telling your story and dissolve the cross-wiring that prevents the inside-out, loving use of sex.

What Kinds Of People Attract You?

The kinds of people you find sexually attractive are examples of cross-wiring that prevent you from finding the mate who would be your most suitable life partner. Harville Hendrix, in

Getting The Love You Want, shows the connections between current attractions and past experiences.

What Feelings Come Up When You Are Sexually Aroused?

Do you feel loved, admired, safe or competent? Are you expressing anger, getting revenge? Do you feel needed? Does the rest of life seem to disappear and lose importance? Any feelings associated with sex and with the anticipation of sexual activity are a rich source of information about cross-wiring. Sorting out the cross-wired feelings from the unfolding love of sexual energy is an involved process — one that is open to continual re-examination and change.

Discovering The Real Nature
Of Sexual Energy

While we are undoing the damage that was done to our sexuality, we can at the same time explore the delights of where we are going. Tasting what we get to have is a powerful incentive to change.

As you play with sexual energy, perhaps with masturbation, see if you feel addictive or expansive and if fear or shame emerges. Become friends with your sexuality. Getting acquainted lovingly will allow you to find out if you are using your sexuality addictively, if you are refusing to use it or if it is sneaking out in ways you haven't been aware of. With compassion for your use of flirtation, pornography, masturbation, fantasy or romance, you can recognize how your sexual energy has refused to go underground. As you invite it out into the open, it can become an ally in your search for healthy sex.

9

Managing Our
Compulsive Behaviors

If you are living with the despair of compulsive and obsessive sexual activity, I know your first question is, "How do I stop?" It is also likely that you have strong feelings of attachment to your activities and you *do not want to stop*. These are important feelings and you can acknowledge them without need for shame. All the information about cross-wiring and the role of our childhoods and culture may be important, but that is the long-term approach. You want to experience a change in the drive that propels you. This chapter takes a look at what you can do right now to lessen the impact of compulsive sexual behavior and obsessive thinking about sexual matters.

First we will work through questionnaires to help you identify exactly what is interfering with your living a normal life. It is likely that your feelings of shame and your double life have actually prevented you from identifying exactly what you do and how you feel. Completing the questionnaires is a first step in bringing your two lives together and reducing the shame you feel about yourself.

While you work on the questionnaires, know that your responses are all yours. You don't have to share them with anyone. It is necessary to give yourself the freedom to put everything down, uncensored. When you are finished, you may consider telling another person you can trust not to shame you — someone who could understand how out of control your compulsions make you feel.

Our long-range goal is to undo cross-wiring, heal from addictiveness and reclaim healthy sexual energy. This process will take time. The first step toward this goal is to come to terms with these behaviors that seem to be running your life. The shame you feel about sexuality and the cultural rule that you mustn't talk about it have kept this part of you under wraps.

As you complete the questionnaire, here are some thoughts to carry with you.

You Do Not Have To Stop

*You do not **have** to stop* doing anything as long as you are not breaking the law. You *get to stop*. If you believe that once you see your behaviors you must force yourself to stop, you may not want to look. Compulsions are not easy to change, as you know. If they were you would have "controlled" them long ago.

Let Your Shame Flow Through You And Out

The shame you feel is not helping you and is actually inhibiting your healing. Shaming yourself will increase your desire to act out sexually. Instead, let the shame flow through and out. (Chapter 10 will give you more information about how to do this.)

Affirm Yourself

Creating your own affirmations to carry with you as you examine your sexuality can contradict some of your shame. Here are some examples:

1. My body is a healthy and sexual container I live in.

2. I have nothing to be ashamed of.

3. I feel no shame.

4. My body, with every fat cell and wrinkle, is adorable and delicious.

5. Every time I act out sexually I am trying to tell my story.

6. I am not my behavior.

7. I am not my thoughts.

8. I was lied to.

9. My life is beginning *now*.

10. I am a whole and loving person.

11. I have nothing to be ashamed of.

12. I am on my path of recovery.

The purpose of an affirmation is to strengthen that part of you that is self-loving and ready to recover. It can also bring up strong feelings that you get to discharge. You will know you have found an affirmation that is right for you if you feel empowered and filled with self-love when you say it. Repeating the affirmation can diminish your shame as you take a took at yourself.

We will begin with questionnaires to identify your behaviors and your feelings about them. Then I will describe Sex and Love Addicts Anonymous groups, the role of acupuncture in the management of your sexual compulsions and the use of aversive conditioning.

Sexual Activities Questionnaire

What are you doing that feels wrong to you? The first step is to identify what is happening with your sexual energy that is causing distress and interfering with the best use of this powerful energy. Take a moment and let your mind explore your sexual activities or lack of them. Embarrassment or shame might come up while you are thinking. If they do, *breathe* air all the way into your lungs and let it flow out and let the feelings flow out with it. Remind yourself that they are just feelings. Feelings are far more painful when stopped up and become tolerable when allowed to flow through you.

Instructions

Read each item and check *yes* for those that apply and *no* for those that do not.

Write in your own words examples or specific activities that apply to you. Add any of your own.

For those items that you check *yes*, complete the rating scale by circling a number from one to five, rating the amount of distress this behavior brings you. One means you have mild discomfort about this component of your sexuality and five is for strong negative feelings.

1. Having sex and then regretting it. (This may be with a lover, a spouse or a stranger. It may be masturbation with or without pornography or fantasy.) Not being able to say no to sex, but feeling bad after it.

NO _____ YES __✓__

In your words: _every hugging feel used made_

myself used –

Mild discomfort				Strong negative feelings
1 _____	2 _____	3 _____	4 __✓__	5

2. Flirting in ways that don't feel clean. Causing or receiving "sexual harassment." Feeling misinterpreted. Being reported by someone who received the flirting. Not knowing what appropriate sexual and physical boundaries are. Being called a "prick tease." Wearing clothes that get sexual attention and not liking some of this attention.

NO __✓__ YES _____

In your words: *Flirting, & not feeling comfortable
& unsure - sexual - frightened*

Mild discomfort				Strong negative feelings
1	2	3	4	5

3. Spending hours in fantasy about sex. (Fantasies may be about a lover, a spouse, strangers, pictures, objects or people you would not have sex with. They may be about children or adults, people of the same or opposite sex, objects or animals. They may contain elements that are troublesome, such as violence or behaviors that violate your values. They may occur while you are having sex or at any time.) "Living in fantasy."

NO __✓__ YES _____

In your words: *Dreams & same day - when
became that is well my expression
control my situations*

Mild discomfort				Strong negative feelings
1	2	3	4	5

4. Devoting more time, energy and money than you would like in preparation for sexual encounters. (This may include excessive grooming, purchase of clothing or gifts. It might involve alcohol and drugs, the cost of prostitution or other sexual attention. It might require time off from work, airline tickets and hotels.) Planning how to interact to get what you want.

NO __✓__ YES _____

In your words: _____

_____

_____

Mild discomfort			Strong negative feelings
1 _____ 2 _____ 3 _____ 4 _____ 5			

5. Being obsessed with thinking about past or future sexual activity. Finding yourself distracted from conversations, work and other activities that you could enjoy if the thoughts would abate. Living in the past or the future.

NO __✔__ YES __·__

In your words: _longing for a relationship_
regretful of past

Mild discomfort			Strong negative feelings
1 _____ 2 _____ 3 _____ 4 _____ 5			

6. Being unable to stop yourself from committing sexual acts that you later regret.

NO _____ YES __✔__

In your words: _I am in my ... duty being involved in places not comfortable to being involved. mind_

Mild discomfort			Strong negative feelings
1 _____ 2 _____ 3 _____ 4 ___✔___ 5			

7. Intensely focusing on a lover, potential lover or past lover. (Attention to him or her that inhibits living comfortably and peacefully in the present.)

NO _____ YES __✔__

In your words: _____

_____

_____

| Mild discomfort | | | | Strong negative feelings |
| 1 _____ | 2 _____ | 3 _✓__ | 4 _____ | 5 |

8. Allowing someone else to determine what you will do sexually and when you will be sexual. (This can be as serious as being forced to have sex, or as seemingly innocent as deciding what you will wear during sex or the order of sexual activities.)

NO _____ YES _✓___

In your words: Afraid to intrate i, be

rejected - unlvrable

_____

| Mild discomfort | | | | Strong negative feelings |
| 1 _____ | 2 _____ | 3 _✓__ | 4 _____ | 5 |

9. Having feelings of yearning, desperation, craving, need or deprivation when thinking about a lover, a potential lover or about being sexual.

NO _____ YES ‾‾‾

In your words: just About that person

extreme dependence

_____

| Mild discomfort | | | | Strong negative feelings |
| 1 _____ | 2 _____ | 3 _____ | ✓ 4 _____ | 5 |

10. Spending time in a trance or altered state of consciousness as though someone else made the decisions. Feeling drugged or euphoric.

NO _✓___ YES _____

In your words: _____

_____

_____

Mild discomfort				Strong negative feelings
1 _____	2 _____	3 _____	4 _____	5

11. Not caring about other people's needs because your sexual ones are too powerful. Letting people wait, cancelling plans, refusing to see friends while engaging in sexual or romantic thoughts or activities.

NO __✓__   YES _____

In your words: _____

_____

_____

Mild discomfort				Strong negative feelings
1 _____	2 _____	3 _____	4 _____	5

12. Worrying about others finding out about your sexual activities or thoughts. Wondering what they would think.

NO _____   YES __✓__

In your words: ___*Objections — Afraid someone*___

___*witting*___

Mild discomfort				Strong negative feelings
1 _____	2 _____	3 _____	4 __✓__	5

13. What has been left out above that is of concern to you? It may be behaviors of others or your own.

NO _____   YES _____

In your words: ___*feelings of numbness —*___

___*much control — S defy the*___

___*person — respond this hard*___

___*ignore my head*___

performing

Mild discomfort				Strong negative feelings
1 ——	2 ——	3 ——	4 ——	5 ——

You now have a beginning picture of what you want to examine while working through this process. To expand your consciousness of what is happening sexually that you want to change, make notes here of specific examples of your experiences that are objectionable to you in some way. Include things that you did and that were done to you. When feelings of shame come up, *breathe.* Open your lungs from your collarbones down to your lower abdomen and let the air flow in fully and gently, and then out.

69

used for someone elses gratification

notch board of door

people have molested before

Feelings About Sexual Activities

Now that you have a picture of what you are doing and the distress it causes, you can look at the distress in more detail. Feelings are important information. They tell you when you want to change activities, and they also tell you when you are using sexual energy in comfortable, loving ways.

I have listed feelings described by people who are healing from addictive use of sexual energy. Some will apply to you and many won't. Some of the feelings you have are very painful and others are only mildly so. This worksheet is designed to help you map out a picture of your feelings and their intensity. Making friends with them so you can listen to their messages is an important step in healing.

Many of your feelings may not be on the list because, even though you have much in common with other people who use sexual energy addictively, you are a unique person. So please add other feelings to the end of the list and use the numbers to rate their intensity.

Instructions

Select a number from zero to four about your level of sexual energy related to each listed feeling and write it on the line after each feeling. Include sexual energy in all forms: sexual arousal, sexual or romantic thoughts, sexual acts and sexual or romantic relating.

0 = none   1 = sometimes   2 = often   3 = usually   4 = always

Ashamed	2	Criticized	
Guilty	2	Possessed	
Lonely	4	Hidden	4
Embarrassed	2	Remote	
Alienated		Removed	2
Humiliated		Not belonging	
Angry		Misfit	3
Resentful		Full	

Enraged	_____	Enriched	_____
Desperate	_____	Wanted	_____
Gone	_____	Loved	1
Safe	_____	Numb	2
Frozen	2	Driven	0
Searching	_____	Crazy	1
Yearning	2	Puzzled	3
Tearful	3	Filled up	2
Starving	_____	Gentle	3
Excited	_____	Delighted	_____
Enlivened	1	Soft	3
Awake	_____	Wondrous	_____
Remorseful	_____	Terrified	1
Apologetic	3	Worried	4
Silly	_____	Impending doom	4
Stupid	3	Obsessed	_____
Compulsive	_____	Sinful	3
Out of control	_____	Controlling	_____

Other Feelings

Feeling	Rating	Feeling	Rating
_____	_____	_____	_____
_____	_____	_____	_____
_____	_____	_____	_____

What Makes Your Heart Sing?

The first two worksheets have focused your attention on what you do sexually and how you feel about it. This is a lot of information to absorb. The next worksheet is designed to help you focus away from your distresses for a moment and look instead at your strengths. This sheet is ready for a list of all those things you like about yourself, your life and your activities. Include everything, not just about sex. Use extra paper or write in the margins, but keep going until it is all down here. If you are in a group, stand up and share your list with great joy.

1. Make a list of what you *do* in your life that you like.

2. Make a second list of what you like about your *life*.

3. Make a third list of all the things you like about *yourself*.

How Do You Increase
Addictive Arousal?

If you are living with obsessions and compulsions, you feel as if they are out of control and they rule you. By looking more closely you will find that the need to avoid feelings of shame, rejection, failure or aloneness leads you to *intensify* the sexual feelings. You are joining with the compulsion to increase the addictive fix. By identifying how this works, you will have more options to interrupt the process so it can't run its course.

First, some background. In the beginning of addiction, sexual feelings themselves are intense and do a complete job of eliminating awareness of anything else. But after awhile, as with mood-altering drugs, the sexual fix doesn't work as well. With sex it is hard to prolong the arousal without some direct stimulation of genitals, looking at pictures or reading books — depending on what your addiction requires.

As time goes on those things that happen at the same time or before a sexual fix become associated with the fix itself and take on the ability to "mood-alter." For example, if the fix is obtained by going to a night club that offers sexual services, the preparation for the evening out can become a ritual that always precedes the event and carries with it the ability to mood-alter. The ritual can gradually extend further back into the day, so in the morning when preparing for work a person might be thinking about the coming evening and feel aroused. People who are romantically addicted can have intense feelings when approaching a date hours or days away. In the euphoria of anticipation, "ordinary" feelings of emptiness or hopelessness cannot be felt. Buying and preparing clothes and grooming preparations can become part of the ritual. With romance rituals, telling people about the person or the date can also be mood-altering.

Kenneth, between four and five on the Continuum of Sexual Addictiveness, wanted his sexual fix when he felt rejected. He often spent several days in a trance state. Only a small part of this time was spent actively masturbating or having sex, and the rest was spent searching for stimuli. He had to find just the right store to buy pornography and just the right street to find just the right prostitute. These compulsions were as important as the sexual activity because they were wired to the avoidance of feelings that seemed intolerable.

When I was in college at age 20, I was at number four on the Continuum of Sexual Addictiveness. I lived from weekend to weekend, waiting for the date and sex that would make my life meaningful. I became amazingly efficient at learning in order to get good grades in spite of my obsession. I walked through a haze of learning in order to get an "education," although I wasn't very educated when I received my Bachelor's degree. My life centered around this man who was my purpose for living. I never once had to think about fears that I couldn't support myself, that I wasn't capable of managing the world. Instead, I had a series of rituals to last through the week, supported by a few hours of sexual contact.

My lover was always on my mind. I was bored with conversation that distracted me from my thoughts. By early in the week I had planned my clothes for the weekend. Every shopping trip was designed to find things to make my body look good. Every shampoo was planned to get my hair to do exactly what it should on Friday night. I structured my studying around the weekend, using the romantic dates as a reward for working hard the rest of the week. I "had to" have a certain amount done before he came to pick me up, and it pushed me into efficiency.

This addiction kept me from feeling the depression I had grown up with and which returned after I married. I later went into psychoanalysis and recreated the romance addiction with my analyst. I lived from session to session, buying clothes and preparing myself to appeal to him — even though overt sex wasn't forthcoming. I was well into my recovery from addictive use of sexual energy before I stopped my rituals. I faced my fears head on, no longer avoiding them with obsessions about finding the "right man."

Ruthie was addicted to masturbation. She would lie in her bed and masturbate for hours, having several orgasms. She became aware that she did this when her life felt empty and thereby avoided feelings of wanting to die. The mood-altering arousal extended into the work day when she thought about masturbating. Her rituals were all in her imagination. They had the effect of making her feel powerful and confident, as sexual energy can do when we allow it to flood through our bodies. She was able to make phone calls and conduct interviews that were difficult for her without the mood-altering arousal. She also attracted men even though she didn't flirt or wear clothing designed to suggest sex. Her constant arousal was stimulating the sexual energy of other people.

Rick used drugs and alcohol to free himself to engage in addictive sex. His rituals included the search for drugs and using them with other people who were also open to casual sexual interaction. The nature of his rituals indicated that his drug addiction was secondary to his sexual addiction.

Returning to your responses on the Sexual Activities Questionnaire and your thoughts about your obsessions, you can take a look at the difference between the addictions themselves and the rituals that have taken on addictive properties. When you can see the rituals that lead to sexual activity, you have an opportunity to interrupt them when they start — an easier time to intervene than during the sexual fix.

Sexual Ritual Sequence

As you look at your responses, put an "R" by those that fall into the ritual category and an "S" if they reflect the sexual fix. As you note which responses are rituals, see if they fall into a *sequence* and think about which ones occur first. The earliest rituals will be the easiest to observe when they are happening and the easiest to interrupt. You may find yourself thinking of more things to add to the questionnaire that can fill out the picture.

Going back over the questionnaire again, rate from one to five the behaviors you have labeled with an "R," based on when they occur in the sequence. Those that come first receive a one, and those that immediately precede the fix receive a five. (Kenneth would give "one" to the initial thought that he wanted to buy pornographic magazines, "two" to the search for the right store, "three" for the decision to go into a store, "four" for purchasing a magazine, "five" for the arousal received while walking and driving with the magazine in his possession. His fix came from looking at the pictures and masturbating, which could go on for hours if the avoided feelings were intense.)

Make a list of all the "ones." Now you have a list of things you do that *begin* the addictive binges. When you see that "one" is about to happen, ask yourself what just happened inside of you or in your life that left you with feelings you wanted to avoid. Practicing this question so it becomes automatic is a vital part of eliminating addictive sexual behavior and gathering the information about directions for your healing.

Telling A Truth

If addictive urges begin because some feelings are arising that seem too uncomfortable to tolerate, one way to stop the sexual feelings is to acknowledge the feeling that you are avoiding. As you become more conscious of your rituals and the beginning of addictive feelings that accompany them, you can identify what was happening just before they started.

For example, when Kenneth got in his car one day to return to work, he found strong sexual feelings and the desire to find pornography coming up. He began the search for just the right store. When this happened, he had already examined his rituals and could see when he began the stereotypical pattern. On this day he backtracked and looked at what he was doing right before the feelings came up. He had gone into a thera-peutic massage center, and when no one was in the outer office he went down the hall to look for someone. A woman scolded him and sent him back to the waiting room with in-structions to wait there. This triggered his feelings of being punished when he didn't know the rules, a humiliating expe-rience from his past. He saw that he wanted to use sexual arousal to avoid feelings of shame as he left the center and began his ritual thinking.

Instead of completing the ritual Kenneth turned his car around and went back to the office. This time he waited for the woman to come out, and then he told her directly that the rules should be posted and he had no idea what she wanted without being told. And he turned and walked out. When he got in his car he had no sexual feelings. He told the truth to her and to himself that there was no need to shame him for what he had done. By telling her the truth he eliminated his feelings of shame and thus had no further need to avoid them.

My sexual and romantic obsession was only put to rest when I found out I could manage the world quite well. I didn't know ten years ago that by acknowledging the fear that I couldn't take care of myself I could have interrupted the addiction. Then I could have faced the fear directly and consciously, feeling its pain. Sexual energy addiction would have lost its function.

Ruthie, who was addicted to masturbation, had to be in ther-apy and address her desire to die before she could give up sex-ual stimulation as a way to feel alive.

Shameless Sharing Of Your Story

The next step is sharing what you have learned with other people who are able to hear you without disgust and without shaming you. Shaming is ineffective in helping us with our behaviors. When we were growing up it only served to drive them underground, and it is no more effective now that we are adults. You have been shaming yourself for some time and it hasn't helped. You will find more help by talking to people who can listen to your story, who know how you feel and who know that letting go of shame is the most powerful approach to allowing you to change your behavior.

I will describe two settings where you can find this kind of non-shaming mirroring — Sex Addicts Anonymous and addictive sexuality group therapy. You can use one or both at the same time. No one will require that you stop your behaviors to be accepted.

Sex Addicts Anonymous

Sex Addicts Anonymous (SAA) (and Sex and Love Addicts Anonymous or Sexaholics Anonymous, depending on the community you live in) is a self-help group based on the 12-Step program of Alcoholics Anonymous. The only difference between the programs is that the addiction is to sexual energy instead of alcohol. S-Anon, the counterpart of Al-Anon, is for the families of sex addicts.

Members of SAA know they use sexual energy addictively and they are actively working on their addictiveness. All of them have felt intense shame because of their behaviors, and they are learning not to judge themselves. One of the 12 steps is welcoming and assisting people who are just recognizing their compulsive sexuality and who are receptive to help. These groups offer a safe, confidential haven for you.

Additional 12-Step programs are available for Adult Children of Sex Addicts and Sexually Dysfunctional Families, and for survivors of incest.

Here's how you can find a group:

The National Sexual Addiction Hotline number is
1-800-321-2066

They will tell you what is available and help you connect with other people who are also addressing addictive use of sexual energy.

You can also write to:

Sex Addicts Anonymous (SAA)
PO Box 3038
Minneapolis, MN 55403

Sexaholics Anonymous (SA)
PO Box 300
Simi Valley, CA 93062

Sex and Love Addicts Anonymous (SLAA)
PO Box 88, New Town Branch
Boston, MA 02258

S-Anon (for families of sex addicts)
PO Box 5117
Sherman Oaks, CA 91413

Adult Children of Sex Addicts and Sexually
   Dysfunctional Families (ACSA)
PO Box 8084, Lake Street Station
110 East 31st
Minneapolis, MN 55408

You can request a brochure which contains a lot of information in a small space. It states the "problem" and the "solution." A list of 20 questions helps you assess your sexual addictiveness. The 12 Steps are listed and information about the organization and its creation are given. Each organization has also produced a paperback book by the same name as the 12-Step program. These can be ordered from the above addresses.

The next step is going to your first meeting. This can be frightening because of the unknowns, and also because you are making a statement that you need help. I believe that when you leave, you will feel better.

New people are welcomed and their discomfort is understood — every member remembers his or her first time. You will be asked to say your first name as each person in the group does, but nothing more is expected of you. You don't have to admit you are addicted to sexual energy and you do not have to talk about your behaviors.

When you are ready you *may* talk about them. The group listens with respect and does not ask you questions or make comments. One of the guidelines is that there is no "cross talking" or discussion of what is said. The meeting is led by a person who has been in the program for some time and who understands the guidelines.

I went to my first meeting to gather information for this book. I was well along in my recovery from addictive use of sexual energy when I first learned there was such as a thing as sex addiction, so I was not able to benefit from these groups then. I thought I would feel out of place because I was no longer ruled by sexual and romantic fantasy, but instead I felt very good being there. The group I attended had about 40 people, too many for a comfortable meeting, so we divided into two groups. I joined the group that addressed "Step One" of the 12 steps, "We admitted that we were powerless over lust — that our lives had become unmanageable." The group was composed of about 20 people, and about half of us were attending our first meeting. We also had some very experienced people who were there to guide the newcomers respectfully into the program.

We began by introducing ourselves by our first names. We were invited — with absolutely no expectation that we must — to talk about our "bottom line behavior," the actions that felt out of control. The experienced members spoke first to demonstrate to us how the meeting went. They explained the limits on describing sexually explicit behavior. (This is so people won't be sexually triggered by listening to others.) They were very frank about what they had done and spoke openly and without shame. Then the new people began to share too. Each person who spoke revealed his or her behavior and feelings of shame. Some people didn't talk and some talked twice.

As this process went on for over an hour, the shame and fear level in the room dropped. Instead of feeling like the only one in the world with a problem, we each saw that other people were also struggling with their sexual energy. A comfort and bonding among members emerged, and by the end of the meeting people were able to smile and look each other in the eye.

I took my turn speaking. I talked about the years of childhood spent in sexual fantasy and the feeling during my recovery that I didn't really have something to recover from. I didn't masturbate or *do* anything that looked like a problem. I couldn't even make a clear statement about my distress. When I was in psychotherapy

I was unable to share my "secret" life with my therapist. As I sat in this group of people, not as a psychologist but as a member, I felt I belonged. There *is* a name for it. I am a recovering sex addict. These people, too, are recovering sex addicts.

Individual Psychotherapy

Working with a therapist may be the best way to start, particularly if you have strong feelings about telling your story. Some people find their emerging shame more tolerable with only one other listener. When your story loses some of its shame, then groups or 12-step programs become easier.

If you find that you need some help retrieving painful information from the past, or the individual support of a person who is comfortable hearing about you, then individual therapy can be a good source of help. A therapist can be an ally to hold on to during the hard work. I recommend that you use all the services you have time and money for — individual therapy, group therapy, 12-step programs and body work.

See chapter 10 for ways to find a therapist.

Sex Addiction Psychotherapy Groups

Sex addiction psychotherapy groups are another place to find help. Groups are usually limited to less than ten people and are led by a trained therapist or counselor. The purpose of therapy includes healing from addictiveness, identifying cross-wiring and unwiring it, and exploring incest. Interactions among group members that reflect other issues are also looked at. A therapy group can become a new family in which to grow up again, this time with consciousness and health.

The presence of a therapist can offer a feeling of safety to get into issues that are associated with intense fear, such as emerging incest memories or feelings toward a lover. Interactions among group members can bring up dysfunctional family patterns and offer an opportunity to work them through. The combination of group therapy and a 12-Step group can be a powerful source of healing.

To find a therapy group in your community, you can begin with the Yellow Pages. Under "Counselors" or "Psychologists" you will find lists of people who offer psychological services. If the ads don't specifically indicate someone who offers groups for people dealing with sexual issues, feel free to call any of the people listed and ask them for information. Part of our job as therapists is to know what is available in the community and provide that information with no charge. I receive such inquiries regularly, and if I don't have an answer I can usually direct a person to where they can find it.

Again, the *National Sexual Addiction Hotline* can also provide you with information about some people in your area. The number is 1-800-321-2066.

It is possible that no such therapy groups exist in your community because the identification of addictive use of sexual energy is new. Few therapists are sufficiently trained or experienced to feel comfortable offering groups.

Acupuncture

During the early part of recovery acupuncture can sometimes help a person who feels sexually driven. When the desire to be sexual is compulsive, acupuncture may reduce the level of sexual energy so it is less available to fuel the compulsions.

Kuo-Ching Yee, M.D., practices acupuncture in Seattle and has published in China on sexual energy. Dr. Yee holds degrees in medicine, physiology and neurology and is a research scientist at the University of Washington, as well as being in private practice. In his 35 years as a physician Dr. Yee has treated many hundreds of people for sexual energy disorders — including impotence, lack of arousal and intense sex drive — with about 70 percent success.

When I interviewed Dr. Yee for this book I was hoping there were some magical acupuncture points that would simply decrease or increase sexual energy. This isn't the case. Dr. Yee explained that he gathers information from the patient to find out the cause of the sexual energy imbalance and then treats this cause.

I have been to three acupuncturists and have found there are different approaches to this healing and different styles among the individuals. While their focus is the physical body, all three attended to all aspects of being human, including the emotional and psychological and the effects of childhood and early adult experiences.

Dr. Yee, from his many years of experience, puts in 10 to 14 needles very quickly. He then puts a small clip on each needle which is attached to a machine that vibrates the needles at changing frequencies. He leaves the patients alone for 45 minutes to an hour with a buzzer to push if they need anything.

I have had wonderful effects from acupuncture on a number of physical problems, including arthritis in my knee. Discussions about acupuncture during these visits brought to my attention the effect on sexual energy.

Dr. Yee talked with me about my own sexual energy, telling me that it wasn't as well defined as it might be. While my channels that influence sexual energy were all fine, he described the impairment as a fog over the picture that kept it from being seen clearly. The picture was clear and good but a "shadow" from the past interfered. He used needles to free up emotion that was still connected to childhood memories. The needles seemed to help my recall of early sexual abuse during the time I was steadily discharging the feelings about it.

Aversive Conditioning

I feel it is necessary to introduce you to some other commonly used methods of reducing the impact of cross-wiring and compulsive behavior, although I do so with reluctance. I have not used these methods. The conditioning of behavior is an approach to addiction that differs from the 12-Step program approach. People in anonymous programs work toward recovery from *addictiveness* rather than toward eliminating certain behaviors.

Aversive conditioning methods come from the behavioral approach to sexual addiction. The methods were developed for use with sex offenders whose sexual addictions are against the law. With these people, election of probation or release from jail may be based on proof that they have changed their cross-wiring and will not commit the same acts.

Aversive conditioning is accomplished by introducing a stimulus that brings about a sexual response and accompanying the sexual response with something unpleasant. This can be electric shock or bad smells or anything the person finds noxious. Ammonia is frequently used. You can create a rotten smell by putting meat in a small jar and allowing it to rot. The 1970 movie *A Clockwork Orange* portrayed this kind of conditioning.

The pairing of two events, a *stimulus* (a "sexy" person, breasts, penises, a child or anything else that is cross-wired to sex) and a *sexual response*, was brought about by some associations from childhood. This is cross-wiring. This pairing is interrupted by presenting a new non-sexual and *noxious response*. The new pairing of stimulus and a negative response (strong negative feelings) interrupts the original pairing and diminishes it. The object is to free the person from the dominating compulsions.

Many behaviorists who work with those whose choice of sex partner is illegal — men who are aroused by children, for example — suggest that the person purchase magazines such as *Hustler* and *Playboy*. The objective is to rewire sexual arousal to socially acceptable stimuli by using pictures of women as sex objects. This is contrary to the Anonymous program's view that *the addiction is to lust*. Changing the object does not change the addiction.

If you are not able to become involved in your recovery, these methods may permit you to move freely in the community without fear you will recommit the offenses. However, if you are actively able to recover and do the hard work to rewire sexuality, then you can employ these methods as only a stopgap measure in the beginning of recovery. If you choose to use them, here is how.

1. *Identify what creates your sexual fix.* Reading romance novels, looking at pornographic magazines, looking at "sexy" people in public or compulsively masturbating to certain fantasies are among the countless possibilities.

2. *Prepare a noxious stimulus.* This can be done by buying ammonia and putting some in a small bottle that can be easily opened and closed to quickly bring on the smell and then shut it off. You can also prepare a more noxious smell by putting meat in a small jar with liquid and some air and keeping it in a warm place for a few days.

3. *Bring about the stimuli.* Get the book or magazine or go to a place you can see people who trigger the arousal. Take your noxious bottle(s) with you.

4. *Pair the smells with the arousal by looking, reading, listening or thinking in ways that bring up your addictive sexual arousal.* As soon as the arousal begins, open the jar and smell. Close the jar. Repeat this eight or ten times and then remove yourself from the stimulus. Repeat this procedure every day for a week. You should

now find a change in the intensity of feeling brought about by
the stimulus and perhaps some other feelings come up when you
are in the presence of the stimuli.

10

Becoming Friends
With Our Feelings

Shame is the primary feeling that addiction is designed to avoid. Altering your mood with addictive activities or drugs makes it difficult for you to feel shame. However, once avoidance is underway you have to avoid more and more feelings because feelings tend to stick together — it's hard to get rid of one without dampening all of them. As you submerge your feelings, another reason for addiction arises — the need to feel again. We can use sexual drive and other intense stimulators in work or recreation, such as fast cars, drugs and management by crisis, so we don't feel dead all the time. What we feel must be intense enough to override the competing desire to submerge feelings.

The deadness brought on by submerged feelings brings about loneliness because we can't feel and we can't connect with ourselves or with others. If we don't combat the deadness with addictive maneuvers, loneliness becomes intolerable. The only true relief from loneliness is the return of real feelings, the route to the real world.

Shame, so well described by John Bradshaw in his book *Healing the Shame that Binds You*, is a pervasive feeling created by abuse of many kinds during childhood. Sexual shaming is the most universal and the kind that has the greatest effect in creating what Bradshaw calls a "shame-based" identity. Shame becomes our basis of identity either by receiving intense shaming in childhood or by identifying with a parent whose identity is based on shame. Both are likely to occur for the child who is sexually abused, compounding the effect.

"Toxic shame," a term created by Bradshaw, refers to a feeling that has no helpful function. In order to recover we must remove the influences of this enemy. To do so requires first that we feel the toxic shame we have internalized. As long as we avoid it, we also avoid the very thing from which we most need to heal. Feeling the shame allows us to find out what beliefs we carry that keep us shaming ourselves. We can return to our painful childhoods armed with the knowledge that the shaming and other violations are wrong — we do not have to believe what we were told and we no longer have to keep secrets.

I strongly recommend reading *Healing the Shame that Binds You*. Using it as a companion volume with this book will allow the greatest understanding of the healing of sexual energy. I found that just reading the book was healing because it makes sense out of the many addictive activities we observe around us. The concept of toxic shame explains the addictive process in our culture. *The shame-based approach to child rearing helps create people who identify with shame and who then use addictive substances and methods to avoid feeling the intolerable shame.*

Because many of us are shame-based, our culture has incorporated addictive behaviors into its fabric. The glorification of alcohol, working hard and sexiness are obvious examples of the ways we avoid feelings. If the social rules say it is okay we are spared further shaming. Society objects only when we carry such activities to an extreme — even though the "extreme" is only the far end of a whole continuum of addictive, shame-avoiding behaviors.

Making Friends With Our Feelings

When we feel victimized by feelings of shame, fear, rage and sadness, one reaction is to avoid or repress the feelings. As long as we do that, we become more addictive and less who we really are. *Addictiveness breeds loneliness and alienation from ourselves and from others — an inhuman existence.*

The route to reducing the need for addictive behaviors is to turn around and embrace our feelings. We can acknowledge that we created our feelings for a reason; they are not evil enemies that we must suffer, mask or eliminate.

Even as we make friends with our feelings, we can know that we want to change much of what we feel and do. Even though we are doing things that are not in our best interest there is no need for shame about ourselves. Of course we want to stop, but shame doesn't help us to do so. *The paradox is that in order to stop feeling shame we must first allow its existence.* We must acknowledge that our intuitive selves are attempting to accomplish something useful with these feelings and behaviors, even though they fail.

In later chapters we will focus on rewiring the cross-wiring from childhood. We will bring to consciousness memories of the past and awareness of current cultural values that inhibit healthy sexual energy. To be useful, the feelings they generate must be available for us to express. Feelings such as being startled, appalled, enraged, terrified, delighted, loved and sexually aroused will come up. As we discharge them, they remove the current that maintains the cross-wiring. As the old wiring falls, it is replaced by a new wiring that comes from the inside out. Befriending feelings at the outset will allow the healing activities to do their work.

Releasing Our Feelings

If we are to allow our feelings to return from suppression, we need to permit them gently back into existence. Holding unreleased feelings in our bodies is stressful and creates many negative physiological effects. Some of the more obvious are headaches, backaches and an overall feeling of tension. It is possible to release these feelings in ways that aren't harmful to us or to others.

Recognizing Our Feelings

The first step is to identify when you are feeling an emotion. If you have spent many years working against awareness, it will take some time. When I am working with clients who aren't aware of their feelings, I ask them what they are feeling several times during a session. At first they cannot answer me, but in time answers begin to appear. If you have difficulty recognizing your feelings, the following exercise may help you to become re-acquainted.

Feeling Alarm Clock

Buy a watch with an alarm or a small portable timer that can be set to go off every hour or so. When the alarm sounds, ask yourself what you are feeling. This will assure that you will ask yourself the question several times a day and begin the process of bringing your feelings back to consciousness. Appendix I has a list of many emotions reflecting the possible variations among the general feeling categories. When your watch signals you, look at the list. First narrow the feeling down to one of the broader categories. Then look at the list within that category and see which word stands out a little more than the others. Ask yourself if that is the right word. Perhaps there is one that isn't listed or a sentence that will better capture what you are feeling. You might want to photocopy this list and carry it with you so it is available when your watch calls your attention to your feelings.

Feeling lessons must include all feelings, not just the ones related to sexual energy. They come as a package, and for a specific one to return they must all be welcomed.

Welcoming Each Feeling

When you have identified the feeling, think of welcoming it — even if you associate the feeling with sexual behavior you don't like or anger with someone that seems unwarranted. For example, the watch alarm sounds and you find yourself immersed in sexual fantasy. As you check the list for feelings, one will be sexual arousal or tension. If you check further, other feelings your sexual arousal was designed to avoid may come up. Perhaps you will find feelings of *shame* for not doing well at work or *anger at your partner* for not providing what you need. It could be *fear of* being found out or *grief* for a loss.

To reach these avoided feelings, you can permit yourself to know that the part of yourself which was trying to take care of you created the addictive sexual fantasy. It was on your side, but like a fire-breathing dragon it destroys even that which it wants to protect. Attempting to slay your dragon will result in further destruction. If instead we can show the dragon that the reality of the present isn't anything like that of the past and ask it to look at the effect of its protective maneuvers, the dragon will be pleased to let go of this all-consuming task of prevention. Pat your dragon and thank it for working so hard to protect you.

As your dragon steps aside, however, you will have to face all those yucky feelings from which it has protected you. Then comes the task of sorting out which ones are the result of cross-wiring and can be changed so you don't have to feel them and which ones are part of being human. These latter feelings, with practice, will become comfortable components of your life. A good searing rage about something we want to change can feel empowering and enriching. Deep grief and despair over the loss of a loved one can allow us to let the person go and get on with our life. Healthy shame and guilt can alert us to activities that are wrong for us and that we want to stop doing from a place of self-loving instead of self-shaming.

If you have managed to stay out of touch with your feelings, inviting them back can be quite a surprising experience. Many people feel as if they are going crazy as feelings flood back and disrupt usual life. You aren't going crazy, you are becoming sane, but in the process you might go through a chaotic time before your feelings settle into more routine patterns. Your feelings are like the jack-in-the-box who is suppressed into a container. When the container is opened he comes flying out and startles you. Once he is out of the box and the pressure is off, there is nothing more to be startled about. The pressure that Jack created is gone and he is no longer pushing against your insides.

Letting Our Feelings Flow

Both the human feelings and the cross-wired add-ons will be tolerable if they can flow through us. When they can't flow through, we must either avoid them entirely with addictive maneuvers or find them stuck in our body in one form or another. Because of this, it is important to be able to let them flow as you embark on your journey of recovery.

If you haven't suppressed all your joyful feelings, think about what happens in your body when you feel love or joy. Looking into a lover's face brings smiles and often sighs. Sighs are deep breaths that allow the feelings to flow. Joy may be accompanied

by laughter. Think about how your body has felt open and fluid
when you were comfortable letting a feeling move in it.

Feeling Release Exercise

To practice the flowing of feelings, begin by bringing a feeling
to mind. For practice select one that isn't too strong. Avoid intense shame for now. You might pick a memory that brings up
apprehension or sadness or annoyance. Before you bring the
feeling up, check out your whole body. How is it feeling? Is there
tension you can let go of?

Check your memory for a time that brought up moderately
uncomfortable feelings that you can recreate in your mind now.
Replay the memory. Breathe deeply. Allow the feeling some time
to emerge. As it comes up, notice where it is experienced in your
body. Take your time. Next, imagine your body is fluid and mo-
bile. Imagine that a cleansing starts, beginning from the top of
your head and moving down your body. Breathe deeply. You are
liquid with feeling, flooding down and down, flowing out of your
feet and down through the floor and into the earth.

Notice the feeling again, see where it resides in you, and
breathe as you allow it to flood down you again, washing through
you, flowing on out of your feet and back into the earth.

Repeat this as many times as you find useful.

Breathing Helps

When we narrow our breath into a constricted space in our
lungs we suppress feelings. Shallow breathing is one of the
most powerful ways we hold feelings back. Learning to breathe
through feelings can counter this restriction. I have observed
this phenomenon countless numbers of times while with clients
in therapy. Usually I become aware of their shallow breaths
when I am also breathing into only a restricted part of my
lungs. I suck air fully into my lungs, freeing them up again.
When I do this some people take it as a cue and will breathe
more deeply with me. As a person breathes again, he or she
gives the feelings under suppression some freedom to emerge.

To begin the process of paying attention to your breathing,
I will give you a specific exercise. As you become more conscious of your body, attention to your breathing will become
automatic, much as your knowledge of when you are thirsty or
hungry is automatic.

Breathing Practice Exercise

Sit in an upright chair, preferably wooden. Notice your sit bones (those two bones you sit on that are cushioned by your buttocks) under you as you bring your body fully upright. By creating distance between your sit bones and the top of your head, you can create space for your lungs to expand. Now allow any tension to fall from your body. Let your shoulders relax and your muscles unwind. As you take your next three breaths, notice the rhythm of your breathing as it is now. When you are ready, fill your lungs all the way up with air and let it flow out. As you do this a second time, check to see if you are expanding all the way from your collarbones down to your pubic bone. Note where the restrictions are. With each deep breath, imagine warmth flooding the restricted areas, allowing them to expand with the air.

I suggest you practice deep breathing every morning when you get up so you integrate it into your being. Breathing deeply is a powerful tool for releasing feelings and for energizing you. Air is the fuel of life, necessary to burn the food we eat in the process of creating energy. "Aerobic" exercise, so good for combating depression and anxiety, is exercise that trains our bodies to use more air in our muscles even when we are sitting still.

Rolfing and some other forms of body work release restrictions that inhibit breathing. They can increase distance from the front of the chest to the back, lengthen the body, and thus increase the room for the lungs to take in air. My lung expansion has increased so much that when I am inhaling with other people, I continue to pull air in after others have reached their limit. Several kinds of body work, including Rolfing, are discussed in detail in Chapter 14.

Now try the *Feeling Release Exercise* again. This time begin breathing deeply and consciously before you bring up the feeling. Notice how breathing loosens up the feeling and allows it to flow out of you more easily.

Finding Others Who Are Befriending Their Feelings

Healing from addictive use of sexual energy and all other sexual issues becomes possible when we have other people who can listen to our stories, feelings and thoughts. Sexual abuse was created in secrecy, and the rule that we can't talk about sex has prevented most of us from unwiring our cross-wired sexuality. The antidote is to *talk* and *talk* and *talk* about sex in the present and in the past, as well as about the rules that dominate it, the attitudes of those around us, the obstacles to talking about it and anything else that comes to mind.

Listening is also a contradiction to those growing-up years when we weren't told about sex in an open, loving way. At last we get to hear all the *real* stories instead of the masked ones that came from adults and the distorted ones that came from peers. We get to find out what is really going on with people's sex lives and to find that there are people who understand our story from the inside out. We aren't the only ones who have difficulties with sex while the rest of the world is comfortably enjoying it. On the contrary, those who work with recovering addicts and co-dependents learn that virtually *all* their clients find they have addictive issues with sex as well.

There are a number of ways to find people who are opening up about sexuality as they recover from the effects of childhood and culture. I will go over each one in sufficient detail so you can decide whether it is right for you and if it is, how to locate listeners. It is possible to participate in any one of these resources or *all at the same time.*

I am among those who believe it is most helpful to *use everything at your disposal.* I find that the people who change quickly and deeply are those who are in therapy, go to 12-Step meetings and get body work at the same time. Twelve-Step meetings provide a network of changing people and a proven course of change steps; therapy offers information about yourself and direction for change; body work softens defenses, makes becoming conscious easier and helps you be aware of what is going on in your body. Three different functions interface to create a powerful path of change.

Anonymous Groups

SAA and other 12-Step groups were discussed in Chapter 9, including directions for finding groups in your community. These 12-Step groups offer far more than help with compulsive acting out. As you become comfortable with the people and develop trust in the process, these groups become one of the most powerful ways to heal.

Talking about your addictive use of sexual activity is the *purpose* of the meetings. Group members know how important it is to tell your story over and over to reduce the shame you feel and to bring your experience out into daylight. A meeting is a powerful place to give up your double life, that sense of being split into two people who are leading separate existences.

Individual Therapy And Therapy Groups

The usefulness of therapy was discussed in Chapter 9. If you decide to seek therapy, here are some ideas:

1. *Phone book:* Call up people listed in the phone book who hold credentials to offer therapy that are approved by the state you live in. Most therapists you call will talk to you personally for ten minutes or so about what they offer and what is available in the community.

2. *Therapeutic approach:* Ask therapists how they do therapy with sexual issues. You might fill them in on what you want. This makes it easier to know how to give you the information you need. I suggest you find out if therapists see their work as consistent with the *12-Step group approach* or focus on *behavior modification/sexual compulsivity approaches*. The latter can provide techniques for managing compulsions and obsessions. However, if you want the full healing from addictiveness and violation of your sexual self that is possible, the behavioral approach does not go far enough. Dr. Ruth's therapy is an example of the behavioral approach to sex therapy — the purpose is to alleviate symptoms rather than reclaim sexuality.

3. *Personal connection:* In addition to an objective appraisal of a therapist's qualifications, another factor — personal connection — is also important. Do you feel a connection with the therapist? Do you feel welcomed? Do you feel you could get help from this person? Do you feel heard? Do you feel respected? (Does the therapist talk to you like an equal human being, provide a comfortable private setting for sessions and waiting space, and communicate clearly the terms of your contract for services? Does the physical space surrounding you feel respected? These elements of respect are particularly important for you when dealing with your sexuality because we know your body and the space around you were not respected during your childhood — our culture does not provide for it. To heal we must have such

respect now to have a mirror of the deficiencies from childhood.) If not, then keep looking. Just because a person has degrees and experience does not mean he or she is a good therapist for you. There is a necessary match, just as with friendships.

When memories of my incest history began to emerge, I saw three therapists before I found one I felt comfortable with. The first was a talented man who used methods that were quite powerful. However, he didn't have a waiting room or even chairs outside his door, and I was required to wait standing up with people passing me on their business. In addition, he was always late and had decided that this was something he couldn't change. On my third visit I stood in the hall becoming angrier and angrier until I realized I was being re-abused and repeating damage from my childhood. As soon as I decided I would no longer see him, my anger and feelings of helplessness dropped. When he came out to get me, I was able to tell him passionately that I wasn't staying for the session, that I wasn't paying for it and why. I felt powerful and self-loving. We talked about it for ten minutes or so and had another conversation a few days later. He realized he hadn't been aware of the effect his choices of office space and time were having on people, and my inform-ing him led to his finding a new office.

My next attempt was with a woman trained as a psychoan-alyst. I walked into her office ready to tell my story, with my feelings waiting to be released once I had good attention. How-ever, she asked me detailed questions, interrupting and effec-tively cutting off my story and my feelings. I watched myself shut down over the first 15 minutes. I told her that her inter-view approach was inhibiting my story, so she put down her pad and said she would listen. Finding it difficult to open up again, I asked her why she used this approach, which I knew was out of character for her training. She acknowledged that she was concerned about the level of feeling I was experiencing and wanted to prevent me from having intense emotional reac-tions after the session.

This allowed me to see that she believed her job was to control the sessions and me, rather than to follow my process. The effect of her maneuver was to leave me feeling more alone and alienated by not feeling heard. She didn't see *me*, a person fully able to feel anything that comes up and be fine later. I was also able to see her react to my questions with discomfort. She could not be the new mother I needed who would allow me to rest comfortably in her presence, hear me, believe me and know at the same time that I was a strong, competent woman.

I found what I needed on my third attempt. I walked into the office of a woman also a psychoanalyst, who had a kind but not concerned look about her. I began my story and knew I had her full attention even when she looked away. I talked uninterrupted for half of the session, and then she joined me in discussing my experiences. She laughed with me at an absurdity that others might not have found funny. I felt seen, heard and respected. I felt at home.

4. *Referrals:* Therapists who deal with incest issues, with survivors of sexual abuse and with sexually addicted people are likely to have developed skills to help you with your issues. If you know people who can refer you to these therapists with some knowledge of their ability and reputation, ask them to do so; this can shorten your examination period. However, it is still important to interview therapists yourself to determine if they are capable of helping you with your tasks.

Twelve-Step programs are a good source of referrals, as are residential programs for drug and alcohol treatment. These centers must know the resources in the community and are willing to share this information with you.

Re-Evaluation Counseling (RC)

I discovered the self-help community of Re-Evaluation Counseling (or co-counseling) several years ago when I lived in Anchorage. I found it to be a helpful resource in my early sexual healing as well as other healing. The concept of early sexual memories and a systematic method for working on them is a powerful aid to recovery. RC offers opportunity to connect with others who are working on sexual healing and provides methods for best use of this connection.

This organization was founded in Seattle many years ago by Harvey Jackins of Personal Counselors. It has been spread throughout the United States by those who found it helpful. Eventually it expanded to other countries.

The basic philosophy of RC is that we are all born fully intelligent, sexual, creative, curious, loving and eager to live fully. These qualities become distorted, hidden and submerged as we respond to hurts brought to us by our environment. By remembering the hurts and having the feelings we couldn't have at the time, we can retrieve our natural human attributes.

Experienced members who have been approved as teachers offer classes that meet weekly for six to eight weeks as well as weekend workshops. The bulk of the work is done by people who meet in twos and threes and small groups to share their memories and feelings.

The purpose of RC is to create a comfortable environment for people to become re-acquainted with their feelings. I was a psychologist when I first took an RC weekend workshop, and I thought I was quite comfortable with feelings. I was amazed, however, at what I learned. I saw that I had given myself and my clients permission to cry as long as it took to relieve the initial distress. During this weekend I saw that the most change came when people *cried for as long as they could!* At the end of the weekend I cried for half an hour straight and felt quite delighted.

At the beginning of the workshop the leader introduced each of us for four minutes. One man stood up with her in front of us and smiled hello. He cried for three minutes, stopped crying and smiled again. I was amazed. I learned from seeing many examples like this that it is possible to *decide when to have feelings.* This man had been able to comfortably set aside his sadness, and then when he had our attention at an appropriate time he could fully discharge it. This approach to feelings is very different from the involuntary holding back that most people in our culture have been trained to do. If our unconscious knows our feelings will be given their time for expression, the effort of holding them in becomes small. It is only when we stuff them, with no permission to ever express them, that we get rages flying out and tears that seem to never stop.

It took me many more months of honoring my feelings before I could do what this man had done. I was in my office in the middle of an afternoon of psychotherapy sessions, and I needed my feelings to be clear and unintrusive so I could attend to the feelings of my clients. I received a letter that I knew was going to evoke many feelings in me. I thought about postponing reading it until the end of my day. Then I realized I could read the letter and save the feelings until later. I did. My unconscious believed that the feelings would have their time and didn't push me. This was quite a lesson for me and proof that the idea we must "control" feelings by holding them in is totally wrong. We can *control feelings by letting them out* — in ways, when and with whom it is right to do so.

If you are interested in learning more about the RC community, call or write to:

Personal Counselors
719 2nd Ave. N.
Seattle, WA 98109
(206) 284-0311

Tell them you want to find out about RC in your area. You will be given the name and phone number of the regional leader who lives closest to you. She or he can tell you what is happening near you. If you live too far to commute easily to classes, it is possible to form a group of people yourself and ask an RC teacher to come to you for one or two days to teach you the basics. When you and your group are ready for a class in Early Sexual Memories, you can do the same thing.

Charges for classes are small and based on a sliding scale. You decide where on the scale to place yourself. Part of this charge goes to the teacher and the rest goes to RC headquarters to support the organization.

Attending Your First RC Class

If you decide to take an introductory class, the teacher will contact you and answer any questions. When you arrive, you will find a room of eight to 15 nervous people, mostly beginners like yourself. Everyone is wondering how this class will go. When I took my second introductory class, I saw how uncomfortable everyone was compared to the end of my first class. I hadn't realized we *all* had been nervous and became comfortable when we learned what the class was about.

It made sense that people would be nervous about taking a class not offered in schools — a class about how to allow your emotions to flow and how to listen when other people are doing the same. This kind of class also allowed us to become comfortable with each other quickly, because we were *real*. We really got to see each other and be seen, which is the definition of intimacy. In this accepting environment we quickly came to value the safety of the group.

Your teacher will have books written by the RC leaders that
you can buy, and copies of a regular publication called *Present
Time* for sale. You might want to buy the short introductory
text prior to the first meeting so you can familiarize yourself
with the principles.

While there is variation in the way teachers handle introductory classes, the following is typical. The class begins with a
lecture by the teacher on general RC theory and practice, the
basic format for the class and how to listen on this first day.
Then the class divides into pairs. Each person talks to their
partner for about six to eight minutes and then listens to their
partner talk for the same number of minutes. Timers are set to
let everyone know when the time is up. The subject is usually
feelings about being in the class.

The class reconvenes as a group and the teacher may lecture
a little more on what will happen next, which is that each
person will have an opportunity to stand in front of the class
with the teacher and talk for six to eight minutes. The teacher,
who is well trained, will do more than just listen — she or he
will help you express the feelings you are working on. This part
of the class brings up fear, and you have the option of not
taking your turn. It is also the power of RC. Standing up in
front of other people when you share your feelings brings them
out of repression. The feeling expressed may be the fear of
standing in front of the room. If that is what is "on top" it is the
feeling to start with. Often having permission to talk about
that fear quickly puts it to rest, and other feelings will push to
be heard.

If it is at all possible, I recommend that you seek the help of
an RC member who has practiced co-counseling for a long time
and who has been approved by Personal Counselors to be a
teacher. If RC isn't available, you will find directions for forming
your own support group in Chapter 13.

Early Sexual Memories

One of the classes RC teaches is Early Sexual Memories. The
class I took was restricted to people who had already completed
at least one class and were familiar with RC methods and philosophy. This was useful because everyone was already acquainted with the boundaries, so we felt safe working together even
though some of us had not met before.

Libby, our teacher, began the class with a presentation of the principles of early sexual memories. She told us that discharging feelings about the earliest memory can release the distress created by later events, so it is helpful to move to the earliest memory as it comes up. We need to tell memories at least ten times to free them of emotional baggage. The memories do not have to seem sexual for a person to be working on sexual issues.

It was noticeable how this group of people meeting on a Saturday afternoon in a living room seemed *bored!* People were yawning and restless and had a hard time paying attention. Yet it was obvious that the subject matter and the presentation were not boring. Libby explained this usually happens during these classes because people are avoiding their feelings about sexual traumas. The results look like a lack of interest.

After her introduction, we paired up and spent a few minutes talking to another person about what we were feeling and began sharing sexual memories. Then we reconvened. At this time Libby stood in front of the group with each of us for ten minutes and supported us as we talked about our earliest sexual memory and allowed our feelings to come up.

Those of us who had been doing co-counseling for a time were accustomed to allowing our feelings to flow through us and out, doing their cleansing work. We were also aware that we could get the best discharge by having more people listen to us talk. So we valued the chance to stand up in front of the group and share.

I had planned to talk about an experience when I was three to relieve the shame I felt for being "caught" in sexual activity. Instead, I found myself talking about a memory from 18 months old that didn't seem sexual. My mother was giving me her "look" and I thought she was preparing to throw me in the trash where I would be picked up by the trash man, squashed into the truck and no longer exist. This "memory" reflected my mother's anger at me for being my father's "lover" and my fear of letting her see me. This memory expresses *emotional incest* even though it did not involve anything overtly sexual.

As I told Libby about my mother putting me into the trash it would have been easy to say this didn't really happen. I am alive so she couldn't have done it. And of course this is right. But what I knew about cross-wiring and imagery told me that *the essence of what I was thinking was correct.* Among my mother's feelings was the desire to get rid of me. She also felt love and protection for me and would not have knowingly allowed anyone to harm me. She wasn't consciously aware that my father was triangulating us, and it was easier to direct her anger at me than at him. She didn't know that at only 18 months I was able to perceive her feelings and be afraid of them.

I learned to trust my feelings, my images and my memories. In another RC session with a couple in their home, I assigned them the roles of my parents and acted like their young child. It was a healing experience to tell them what I needed and see them smile and love each other as they responded to my needs — until the woman said she was baking bread and needed to tend to it. I felt a wave of panic. My skin puckered and I gasped for air. I didn't invent this feeling. It didn't come from the man who was playing the role of my father. It came from my childhood where I was afraid to be alone with my father because I could not say no to being used sexually. This role-play situation I had created brought up these feelings from my past and allowed me to become conscious of them. Years before when my feelings were submerged and negated I would have thought I had made it up or read it in a book. To do my sexual healing, I had to know that the feelings may not be appropriate in the present, but I *did not make them up*. They had a significant origin.

Using Arousing Fantasy

Another way RC early sexual memory work unwires cross-wiring is by beginning with a present fantasy instead of a memory. We can assume that sexually arousing fantasies, video scenes, book plots or certain sexual activities that feel driven have some relationship to our past. By telling the fantasy or scene and allowing the feelings of shame to flow through us and out, we can discharge enough of the tension around the scene to be able to use it to learn about ourselves. When we can tell it and see that people are listening, it becomes a source of memory for the events that created the cross-wiring that it expresses.

When I have worked on sexual images and body positions, I find that I initially experience cross-wired sexual arousal. However, once I begin telling about it the arousal drops off and the hurts that created it emerge instead. With a few tellings, the arousal doesn't return and the whole character of the image changes. It loses its power.

You may find after telling it that a favorite fantasy doesn't arouse you any longer and that your sexual energy will come from other sources. Some people worry that if they are no longer aroused by their fantasy they may not find anything to arouse them. Instead, a different kind of arousal becomes possible, one that is only available as the cross-wiring fades. It is more gently aroused, more deeply passionate and more consuming of the entire being. This is in contrast to the intense, driven quality of the fantasy-aroused sexual feelings that are so strong they serve to *avoid an awareness of the self.*

An important component of RC and any healthy unwiring process is the right to say *"no,"* refuse to participate and have our feelings about safety and boundaries. The feelings "on top" are always the first to be addressed, and if those feelings are fear about what is happening they need to be discharged first. Healing from sexual child abuse requires reclaiming the ability to say no to contradict the powerlessness of childhood. It is valuable to be able to scream, "No, no, no!" and have others respect it.

If you want more help in reclaiming your feelings, sex-related and otherwise, I highly recommend the RC organization. You will find joyful, free focus on feelings and the resulting ability to truly accept them as a natural part of human life.

The costs for groups and weekend workshops are small, and there is no cost for the unlimited additional time spent sharing with other members of the class. The classes and weekends offer the opportunity to meet other people you would like to work with in pairs or small groups so you can have several "co-counselors." These are people who will listen to you with caring and with no judging. The cost of this attention is your listening time — you give them the same accepting listening time.

Meeting With Co-counselors

The instructions for meeting with co-counselors are specific. The relationship is not a friendship and will not become one. However, those who are already friends remain so. An appointment is set and the amount of meeting time agreed on. This time, which can vary from 20 minutes to two or more hours, is divided evenly among the people present. A timer is used so no one has to keep track. For example, when I met with Eileen, we planned to meet for 90 minutes and divided that time into two

45-minute sessions. When three of us met, as we did for early sexual memory work, we divided the 90 minutes into three parts. We decided who would begin, and the other person or people listened intently while the first person talked.

When working on early sexual memories, we told the earliest memory and then told it again. We encouraged each other to discharge our feelings, knowing this was more important than the telling. Sometimes one of us would cry for 20 minutes or more without saying much or pound pillows with a racquet. We didn't have to know what the feelings were about, although we usually found out pretty fast once they were flowing.

Giving Ourselves Permission
To Discharge Feelings

Feelings express themselves through our bodies, so allowing our bodies to be clear channels for them is important. I have described how shallow breathing is a way to hold feelings back. As we learn to give our bodies permission to breathe, we can also give them permission to tremble in fear, blush in shame and yell in rage. Tears and sobbing express sadness and despair. Tears seem to be acceptable in many quarters, but sobbing while your face squeezes up like a crying infant's seems to be harder on uninformed listeners. They often think you are going crazy and that they must help you stop. It is, however, very effective.

The first time I was alone when I cried like that, I looked at my face in a mirror to see if I looked really ugly. I didn't! I looked rather odd but also quite interesting. One of the benefits for me from RC was getting to see other people do these odd things that I never saw growing up. These were normal, well-functioning people who held responsible positions in the world. Using this criteria of being "acceptable" from my childhood, I could bring my two realities into one and see strong, discharging emotion as part of life.

Yawning deeply is also a discharge of emotion, as is laughing. Often when my therapy clients want to laugh at something that isn't funny, they feel shame and hold back the laughter. I encourage them to laugh to release the top of the intense emotion. Laughter can dissolve into tears or fade into anger.

Laughter is also an expression of joy, of course. Joy and delight and enthusiasm are also emotions that *need* to be expressed. While these feelings don't receive the cultural disapproval that the "negative" ones do, we are still quite repressive even in our joy.

Ideally we could have grown up with permission to use emotional discharge while out in the world, but since we haven't, we have to consciously reintroduce our feelings. My first experience with this was a powerful lesson.

A friend who also co-counseled gave me a spontaneous RC session while driving to a mall to go Christmas shopping. I asked her if I could do a brief session, and she said yes. (It is always important to ask permission to set aside the normal social boundaries and to ask your co-counselors to give you their full attention.) I began to yell. I was preparing to purchase presents for my sister's family, whom I seldom saw. She had not supported me in a family crisis a few weeks before, and now I was out spending time and money on a holiday obligation. As I yelled about it, I became clear within minutes as to my feelings toward her and giving gifts out of obligation. I made some important decisions about Christmas that have remained with me.

I gave my friend the choice of taking equal time then or keeping track of the time which she could use later. She chose the latter because she preferred to continue with her shopping plans.

Rex and I have integrated permission for expression of feelings into our relationship in two ways. One, we ask permission to express our feelings. If the other is able to listen at the time, the feelings are allowed to flow out without evaluation of their rationality. As the discharge becomes complete, clarity comes quickly. We use the second method for feelings that feel directed toward each other even though we know the other hasn't caused them. We hold our fingers up beside our ears as if they were another mouth speaking. We call this mouth our "inner voice," which we know comes from our unconscious or our child selves who made up rules about the world long ago. This signal helps us know that the other isn't truly blaming or yelling at us.

I used this method to reach clarity one day when I got home from a trip. Rex had held a Rolfing workshop in our home while I was gone, and several people had slept at our house. This seemed like a terrific arrangement until I walked in the door. The living room was disorganized, not returned to its original state after the workshop. I felt rage flood over me and simultaneously the push to hold it back because it didn't make any "logical" sense. I also knew my feelings were likely to trigger

Rex's shame because he was in charge of the house while I was gone. Nevertheless, being true to our agreement to share *everything*, with full feeling, I put my hand up to my ear, indicating that my "inner voice" needed to speak. At the same time I looked at him quizzically, asking if he would agree to hearing my rage. He nodded.

And I started in. "This is *my* house! Things aren't where they are supposed to be. I leave for five days, and I come home and it isn't my house any more. Tell me what happened here. What did you let them do?" I stormed into the kitchen, seeing more things out of place. "Did you tell them they couldn't eat here? *They cooked here!* They cooked in my kitchen and left their food in *my* refrigerator!" I began to jerk out the leftovers, and fling them into the trash. Then the ultimate — there was *beer* in the refrigerator. We don't allow alcohol in our home and don't interact with people who are under its influence. So to find alcohol in the kitchen was the final straw in my raging demand for respect of my boundaries. The beer followed the food into the trash.

I felt *wonderful!* The rage flowed through me and out, leaving me feeling cleansed. I hadn't hurt anyone, although I wondered if the neighbors could hear me. They would have interpreted my raging as screeching at my husband and being quite unfair. And if I were blaming him, it would have been unfair.

But Rex was taking all this in with delight. After an initial wave of shame, he could see that I was expressing his feelings about all this, too. His co-dependent rules of "niceness" had kept him from setting limits in our home that he also wanted, while I had the freedom of arriving after it was all over. I was his mirror for the isolation he had felt during the workshop because he cut himself off from the people in order to be "nice." They, of course, had no idea he was upset by their taking over his house. They were "making themselves at home," as they had felt invited to do.

The next workshop he held alternated between our offices and our home, and I worked in the space he wasn't in. This time Rex sent guidelines to the participants before they arrived and put notes up to make it clear which rooms were used for what. Some of the people had been to the first workshop, and they tested these limits but responded to Rex's reminders. Both of us felt comfortable sharing our home and office space with people when we were able to be clear about our limits.

My rage was a signal that I wasn't setting boundaries I was comfortable with. It gave me a chance to make changes that allow me to interact more comfortably with others. In years past I would have felt compelled to follow the rules of society about "hospitality" and open my home in ways I didn't want to. I would have converted my anger into silent hostility, probably directed at Rex, and I would have found excellent "reasons" why no further workshops would be offered. Rex would have been angry with me and we might have argued over this, unable to come to resolution. As it turned out, Rex and I and the other Rolfers all got our needs met by making a few changes.

By permitting this rage to surface, I was using it as a valuable source of information. Having nondestructive ways to allow my anger to flow through me allowed me to learn about it instead of reasoning it away or inhibiting it with shallow breathing. When we can do this with all of our feelings, we have the information we need to know how best to live.

Co-dependency Classes And Groups

Co-dependency, the addiction to people or to addicts, is the subject of 12-Step groups and therapy groups that are increasing rapidly. Millions buy books on the subject, and the word "co-dependency" is becoming a common term. As a result the possibility of finding classes and groups that deal with it is increasing, even in moderate sized communities.

Co-dependency groups provide the opportunity to express feelings and study addictive behaviors in a community of other people who are doing the same. The 12-Step program is called CODA (Co-dependents Anonymous) and the 12-Step principles are usually part of therapy groups for co-dependency.

These groups are not oriented specifically to the addictive use of sexual energy and are often not knowledgeable about the subject. It is usually better to find groups that are.

In your search for co-dependency groups use the same methods I described for finding a therapy group. Call up professionals and ask them for information. Treatment centers for chemical dependency will certainly know what is available.

Recovery With Your Partner

If you are in a relationship with a person who would also like to heal his or her addictive use of sexual energy, you have the opportunity to enter a powerful arena for change. Do not try to heal alone, however. The volatility of intimate relationships makes them a risky place to bring up old memories and current feelings. We project our needs and dependencies onto our partners, so the chances of having intense feelings of criticism, jealousy and possessiveness are high. With the help of the resources listed previously and by forming a network of recovering people, you can create the necessary safety to work together. Please see the guidelines and boundaries recommended in Chapter 13 for starting a support group. These same guidelines can make your relationship with your partner emotionally safe.

Friends Who Are Also Healing — Create A Support Group

You can create your own support group by finding other people who are interested in healing their sexual energy. One way to connect with other people is by lending this book to those you know and see who shows interest in discussing it further. When you have four to eight people you can form a group and use the information from this book. Chapter 13 gives instructions for beginning a support group with other people who want to unwire their cross-wired sexual energy. Or you can form a 12-Step group by writing to one of the headquarters for information about how to do this.

11

Telling Our
Stories

Our culture dictates that we cannot talk about sexual issues. The discomfort is visible when a group of people sit down to do just that. Even a group of psychologists I taught who work with incest survivors spoke in very low voices as they shared a small part of their sexual experience. When people do talk, it is usually with innuendo or jokes or indirect references to sexuality.

Along with not talking about sex, we repress most of our childhood experience of it. As Alice Miller describes so well in her book *Thou Shalt Not Be Aware,* we all agree not to remember the childhood abuses of our sexual energy. Most people who have not had therapy say they have little memory of their sexuality before puberty. The memories stay repressed until they are invited to come back. The invitation must be strong to overcome the rules that our unconscious adopts from our culture. You can use the methods in this chapter to invite your repressed memories to make themselves known and to offer them your belief and respect.

As long as you can't talk about sex or retrieve memories from your unconscious, you limit the possibility for changing the effects of your cross-wiring. Talking, on the other hand, can bring out your stored memories and allow you to discharge the feelings that are trapped with them. Telling your memories again and again, along with the feelings, allows them eventually to be remembered as just facts — no longer the highly charged sexual arousers they once were. The natural rewiring will happen automatically. So let's talk.

Safe Environments For Discussing Sex

By deciding to talk about a forbidden subject, you are opening yourself up. Most other people will continue to adhere to the cultural rule not to discuss sex and not to remember sexual history. They will try to prevent you from making them uncomfortable. They will give all the reasons you heard growing up as to why you shouldn't talk sex. Many may sound plausible. A therapist with several years' experience objected to my "Sexually Speaking" workshop for psychologists because she said some things just shouldn't be talked about and talking about sex removed its mystery.

A safe environment can support you while learning to talk openly about sex. Here are some possible ways to create one.

See A Therapist

An individual therapist who is knowledgeable about sexual issues, incest and the importance of our childhood and culture can provide the safest place to begin. See Chapter 10 for information about selecting a person who can be the most help to you.

Join A Therapy Group

A therapy group designed for discussion of sexual matters is a place where the therapist creates safety. This is also true for 12-Step groups and RC groups because they are led and the ground rules are clear. Joining such groups is a valuable way to begin.

Find People Who Want To Talk

When you venture out to talk with people outside group settings, you can design your own limits. When approaching people who are not already involved in talking about sex, begin by *telling them what you are doing*. Ask if they are interested in pushing against the "don't-talk" rule with you. If they say no, move on. People who aren't willing to examine their sexual damage will not be good allies. They will be invested in maintaining the rule and will try to get you to do the same. They cannot hold accurate mirrors for your discoveries.

People who can join you will enrich your life by broadening the environment in which you feel "normal." As we talk to others about all the sexual things in this book, from our childhoods to our families, to our culture and our current sexual activities, then we become part of the cultural shift that is underway. We can join together synergistically to violate the old rules that have kept us prisoners. We can bring our knowledge out from under repression and allow our wisdom to be available to us. *We can't do all this alone.* We need a community of people who are also retrieving innocent sexual energy. Our culture will shift only when we can talk freely to people everywhere. We will know our culture has shifted when we encounter a person who is still of the old way of thinking and their ideas seem strange!

A member of one of my therapy groups gave us a wonderful example of taking healthy sex out into the community. Jess, a single man about 30, is a member of a strong church congregation. After about three months in group, he was at a church picnic where the subject of sex was hinted at in our culture's usual indirect fashion. Jess saw what was happening and with his warm smile and straightforward manner just said, "Sex is really good." He noticed that the adults were uncomfortable, but the children seemed amazed and interested to hear this grownup speaking this way. He asked them if they knew about sex and they nodded. He repeated that sex is good and then joined in other conversation. It is unlikely that these children had ever heard an adult speak of sex in an open, healthy way. They have a new imprint to carry with them as they move into young adulthood.

Jess was using his new community of the therapy group to expand the environment in which he feels comfortable speaking about sex. And the effect rippled. Only four months earlier, when Jess signed up for my four-week class, he had been almost unable to say that he masturbated. He believed he was the only one. Telling his story and hearing the stories of others dramatically changed his understanding of typical sex lives.

As we are speaking up about the forbidden and the "unknown," the more we have a sense that this is common stuff everyone else deals with too, and the easier it is for information to ease out of repression and into the everyday. For this reason, I encourage you to explore the boundaries of a variety of people in your life to find those who can form your new community. We are the *"We Shalt Be Aware"* generation.

One way to approach people is to ask them if they have heard of this book. If they haven't, you can tell them some of the ideas, which allows you to begin with intellectual discussion. This is not as risky as telling part of your own story. If your listener shows interest then you might take another step and reveal something more personal about your sexual history or present life. I would suggest choosing something with little risk to begin with and then increasing the risk when you see the other person isn't going to shame you.

Other people will have a variety of reactions to your initiation on the subject of sexual energy. Some will be fascinated and want to talk, but most will feel discomfort. Many will not want to violate the Thou Shalt Not Be Aware commandment and will shame you for doing so. Others will want you to stop because they do not want their own sexual issues to come out of repression. Survivors of incest who are not yet conscious of it will be threatened by someone who can talk openly. Still others will suspect your motives. People of both sexes may think you are trying to initiate a sexual interaction because you are violating a strong boundary. We have maintained artificial boundaries by saying nothing about sex with people we don't want to have sex with, so when you step across the boundary some people will react with fear. There will also be those who will experience an unhealthy interest in the subject and use the discussion addictively. You may feel discomfort with the person's reaction, and choose to end this discussion. Talking is *essential* for the necessary cultural shift that will allow all of us to reclaim our healthy sexual energy.

Form Your Own Group

When you find people who want to join you to bring this subject into the arena of ordinary conversation, the next step is creating ground rules to make the situation safe. It will be a long time before we are able to see sex as ordinary conversation. Chapter 13 details the group structure that can give freedom to each person to explore the forbidden. An important limit to set is the prohibition of sexual interaction between people. All stimulation should come from inside of you, not from the outside, and you need a guarantee that you will be free from intrusion. At this point a rule can help because few of us know when we are being intruded upon sexually. While we were growing up our boundaries were not respected. Safety from flirting and more overt sexual suggestions provides an environment with boundaries that didn't exist when we were small. Imposing the boundary of *no sexual contact* can free us of the need to decide what is and isn't appropriate.

If your partner is in the group, then of course this rule of no sexual contact doesn't apply when the two of you are alone. The boundary is still important, however, while you are doing the emotional work of remembering and feeling, whether you are alone with your partner or with other people.

Other guidelines are:

• Maintaining confidentiality.
• Listening without interruption.
• No judging.

These are discussed in Chapter 13.

Allowing Shame To Come Up And Wash Out

Shame is the major enemy of the decision to talk and of retrieving memories. The culturally prescribed shame when talking about sex and the childhood shaming you inevitably received around your body and your sexuality join together in an attempt to get you back in line. Letting these feelings come up and flow out can open doors to freedom.

Breathing fully will keep feelings flowing more easily. Shame is just a feeling. You are alive, and shame can't stop you. Breathe in life and exhale shame and fear. Again and again.

When other people are talking you may find your cultural sanctions interrupting. You also have rules that they mustn't talk about sex. You can release feelings of fear and shame that accompany listening with breathing and sometimes tears. As others speak let your feelings flow and you can both benefit.

Telling Our Sexual Histories

When approaching this area of humanness we have believed off limits, I find the RC format to be excellent. It establishes boundaries within which we are free to allow anything to emerge. As paradoxical as it sounds, tight boundaries enhance freedom. Chapter 13 details how to establish a group and the boundaries that create safety for members so they can speak of unsafe things.

When I am working with someone in therapy and invite him or her to talk about sexual history, it is usually the first such experience for the person. Thoughts, feelings and new awarenesses come up as the memory expands through telling.

When you are sharing your sexual history, allow yourself to ramble on about events that may not even seem related. Allow the story to emerge out of you with no requirements for types of events or their order. Your unconscious will want to trick you out of doing it and will make you think you are bored or sleepy or boring your listeners. It may also get you to talk about things that truly aren't related to your sexuality. As you let this happen, you can assess whether you are avoiding something painful.

Rick began therapy because his "live-together" relationship wasn't working well. He soon learned that his sexual longings for a man's penis and his addictive behaviors around that longing were the primary issues he wanted to address. As we looked at his sexual history, which initially did not include memory of sexual abuse, things began to shift for him. Expressions of surprise and puzzlement appeared repeatedly as he talked because the memory looked and felt so different when spoken to an attentive listener.

He began talking about the first time he had sex at age 16, believing this was the beginning of his sexual history. As he went on from this unsatisfactory event to his first relationship, he was able to release feelings of shame that accompanied his lack of awareness of his partner. He felt he used her for sex and the safety of bonding without really knowing who she was. He abandoned her when he moved on to a relationship with a man. As he was able to see the abusive treatment he gave and received, we began to search for memories of childhood abuse. His shame lowered and the memories arose.

One morning when he was sitting at breakfast with his wife, an image came to mind. He saw himself lying on his father's bed next to his father. His father's penis was erect and out of his shorts, and Rick was sucking on it. He was appalled, and immediately discounted the memory as purely his imagination. As he related it to me, I told him it was unlikely he could make up such a scene. It was the obvious precursor to his desire to find a man who would be the loving father that would allow him to suck his penis. In the scene, his father touched him affectionately and focused intense attention on him — the only time in Rick's memory.

The next information that emerged out of repression related to his mother. As is often the case, the sexual contact itself was not the most damaging effect of the incest. Rick felt his father's shame over their sexual interactions and knew without being told that he must keep this from his mother. He consequently felt dirty and disgusting in his mother's presence, believing she would throw him out immediately if she knew the truth. As a result, he didn't have the comfortable security of either a mother's or father's love. His mother didn't know what was going on with him, believing he was just a strange, reclusive and angry child by nature.

His anger over this situation manifested in passive-aggressive, indirect ways of behaving throughout his young adulthood, causing further rifts between him and his parents. By this time he didn't know what he was angry about because he had repressed the incest.

He turned to drugs to medicate his rage. After years of LSD, alcohol and marijuana, he developed an addiction to cocaine that forced him to recover from his addictiveness. He dealt first with the substances, then with his sexual addiction and then came upon the reasons for all of them. As he faced the abuse he experienced as a child, sexual and otherwise, his general addictiveness declined. The lesser addictive behaviors had included compulsive shopping, watching movies, staying busy, gambling and compulsively working long hours to pull himself out of debt. His mind gradually cleared, and he was able to create a life including information from the past and expectations of the future that no longer fed his addictive behaviors or made them seem valuable.

Rick was able to do this work by talking about his sexual history, even though initially he had no memories of sexual activity before age 16.

We have different kinds of memories. Some of them are just under the surface and you will feel surprised that you hadn't thought of them before. People respond to these retrievals as if they really had remembered but just hadn't thought of them for a long time. These memories will have pictures and words to accompany them, and are obvious memories once you speak them.

Other memories seem to be made up or are like fantasies. You might want to say that you must have read them somewhere, that they didn't really happen. *If you can suspend judgment* and act as if they are real, the truth can eventually emerge. Thus, memories may change, or you will get to see their value to you. While the memories may or may not be literally true, they contain truth.

My memory of what happened when I was about 18 months old didn't really happen the way I first told it. I said that my mother put me in the trash, the trash man came and took me away and I was disintegrated in his truck. Since I am alive today, I could have said that I made this up or saw it in a movie, but I didn't. I suspended judgment until it became clear that this was an early sexual memory. It had to do with my mother's rage at me for being the object of my father's sexualized attention. She couldn't let herself know that his sexual energy was focused away from her, so I became the receptacle for her rage over his lack of monogamous bonding with her. I felt in constant danger of being destroyed and my child's mind constructed the manner by which she would do this. She got rid of unsavory, rotten, smelly things in the trash, so I figured she would put me there as well.

Telling Our Early Sexual Memories

The following are guidelines for the process of working on your early sexual memories.

1. *Begin with the earliest sexual memory you have in your consciousness,* which could be at age three days or 30 years. Telling memories about sex is valuable even if it was only yesterday's experience. As you begin talking more memories can come to the surface.
2. *Tell the memory slowly.* The primary objective is to discharge feelings that accompany the memory. If you spend all your allotted time crying and saying very little, you have made excellent use of your time. If you override the tears to complete the "task" you will be deprived of the cleansing effect of talking. You might not finish telling your memory the first or even the fifth time through.
3. *Allow the shame to come up.* Letting shame, fear and other feelings associated with the memory come up is the purpose of this exercise. Breathe and let the feelings flow.
4. *Tell the memory a minimum of ten times* before you expect it to be clear of shame. After the first telling, celebrate your ability to retrieve it and tell it to someone else.
5. *The memory becomes more believable to you with each telling.* Memories that are newly out of repression seem made up or the result of an active fantasy. Over a period of weeks or months, the memory can firm up and feel as though it really did happen to you.
6. *Telling your memories with two or more other people* present feels safer than talking with only one person. This is because most of our abuse occurred with one person and we were unable to go to a second person for protection and safety. Meeting with two people contradicts the immobilizing fears associated with talking about sex when you were young.

   There is also an element of actual safety here. None of us has completely clear sexual boundaries, so it is possible for one of your listeners to violate your boundaries accidentally in subtle ways. If this happens you have another person there whose presence makes you safe. You don't have to figure out what your limits are and explain it to your listener.
7. *Meeting on a regular basis* can prime the memory pump. Your unconscious holds the awareness that you will search it again at a specified time, and this knowledge can stir around in your memory traces.

Telling Our Sexual Fantasies

Sexual fantasies — which include pornography preferences, sexual thoughts and images we create when having sex or masturbating — are a powerful source of information about the causes of cross-wiring. Telling these fantasies can open doors to early sexual memories that cross-wired our sexual energy, giving us the opportunity to unwire them.

As you tell your fantasy, pay attention to your feelings. Shame and fear from telling can be expressed in the same way as with early sexual memories. *If any sexual arousal begins to come up, this is very valuable information.* As soon as it does, you can know you are onto something that happened to you when you were young. Tell that part again, staying with it, and wait to see if anything more comes up. If memories or thoughts appear, tell them too.

Kathryn told her therapy group the fantasy that created intense arousal when she was masturbating. A person was in front of her wearing armor-like clothing, so hidden that it wasn't clear if it was a man or woman or what the person was experiencing. The person stimulated Kathryn with a vibrator-like object until she had an orgasm. He or she expressed no feeling or even awareness of Kathryn. As she talked, Kathryn began to cry as she saw how impersonal the sexual interaction was that seemed to bring pleasure. She talked about the way her father removed himself from the family in order to protect himself from being entangled in the crazy web created by her mother. His remote but sexualized interactions with Kathryn were converted into this. Her arousal was cross-wired from the love she wanted and the sexualized distance she received.

Tapping Body Memories

Our bodies store memories that our brains may never be able to reveal in words and pictures. We have a record of every physical thing that was done to us, and we can learn to tap into this record.

One way body memory appears is when we are being sexual, as Anna's preference for anal stimulation demonstrates. Her body remembered, from childhood sexual abuse, that her anus would feel less pain when penetrated if she were sexually aroused. She associated anal stimulation with rapid, intense sexual arousal and used this in adulthood to create arousal. As she came to respect that her body was expressing her cross-wiring and remembered exactly what happened to her, she was able to retrieve awareness of the form of sexual abuse she had received as a baby. Her cross-wiring cleared and she discovered that inside-out arousal was different from that provoked by cross-wired anal stimulation.

During our daily activities our bodies also reflect our childhood experiences. People who have had penises put down their throats can find themselves frequently clearing their throats, experiencing tightening of the throat when under stress and having difficulty swallowing pills. Sucking on your mouth, especially when under stress, can be an attempt to express the sucking reflex experienced when a penis was put in your mouth as a baby. Some people report sucking until air is pulled past their lips, making a sound that alerts them to what they are doing.

Jean found herself with a strong aversion to penises in her adult life and believed that both her husbands caused her distress. As she worked on her memories, she found she had been forced to touch her father's penis and to withhold her objection. She told of lying behind her husband when he reached for her hand to tuck her arm around him. He accidentally brushed her hand against his penis and she experienced an involuntary jerking away of her hand. Startled by her reaction, she took advantage of the situation to make the connection that she hadn't been able to pull away when she was very little. She came to hate penises so she didn't have to hate her father for what he was doing to her. Her hand remembered the feel of a penis and the desire to wrench away. She is now able to respect her hand's memory.

While May and I listened, May's body told the story of her sexual abuse. Over a period of about 15 minutes she described what she was feeling in her body. Before she started talking, we knew that she had been abused in childhood because *all* her childhood pictures from the age of six months on carried an angry, hurt expression. We didn't yet know that the abuse was sexual.

First she was aware of a choking sensation as though someone had their hands around her neck. Then her head felt pulled to one side against her will. Her stomach felt pressured. Her mouth fell open, and her jaw experienced intense pressure and then pain. She was literally feeling the pain as she spoke. Her throat constricted and she gagged. This was followed by the feeling of liquid running down her face from her mouth and the sensation of having it wiped off. This was accompanied by intense sexual arousal approaching orgasm.

Over the 15 minutes of the telling, it became clear to both of us that a man had put his penis into her mouth, ejaculated and then cleaned up the evidence. She had been sexually aroused in the process. We knew the look on her baby face was anger about not being protected from this treatment and outrage that it had happened.

After we discussed the meaning of the body memories, May turned her anger on me. She said I had planted the seed for this experience and that it wasn't her memory at all. I sat quietly, knowing that she needed to direct her distress where it was safe to do so. Her body told the story, but she wasn't quite ready to hear it. She could prevent the full impact of the memory by finding another explanation for it — that I had made it up. At the same time she knew I hadn't and she was terrified of knowing all of what had happened to her. Every three to four sessions she retrieved more memories through her body and then with picture images. Over extended time she became strong enough to know that these things really did happen to her and that her body had remembered.

Three years before coming to see me May had received the ten-session series of body work called Rolfing that realigns the physical structure and tends to accelerate change people are ready for. Since that time she had found intrusive feelings and thoughts penetrating the carefully designed, pleasant mask that covered the outraged child face she had shown until her late teens. Rolfing touches the body deeply and can reawaken memories held in it. (See Chapter 14 about body work and other ways to allow your body to speak more clearly to you.)

As you learn about your body and respect its messages, you can better listen to the memories it tells you.

Using Our Power Of Visualization

Instructing our mind to imagine certain things and then asking it what comes next is a powerful way to circumvent our unconscious and get it to tell us things that it won't with direct questions. I use guided imagery with classes and groups and in individual therapy sessions to help people gather more information.

In this chapter I will demonstrate one example of imagery that I have found useful in classes. You will find a series of other examples in Appendix II that you can choose from for specific situations. As you become familiar with this way of gathering information, you can make up your own imagery.

Some of my clients allow their story to unfold with no outside prompting. Most people, however, value guidance that gives permission. You can ask someone to guide you in imagery you know would be useful, or you can make your own tape and play it back to yourself.

You can do the following imagery alone, or one member of your group can read it slowly while everyone else closes their eyes and follows the directions.

Instructions For Reading The Imagery

Here are some things I have learned about how to read an imagery aloud when in a group. Read slowly in a soft, gentle voice. Your listeners will be moving into an altered state of consciousness and you want to help them do so. Normal conversational tones will bring them back to the present.

The dots indicate times to wait while your listeners allow their images to unfold. Each pause should last a *minimum* of ten seconds, and it is helpful to wait 30 seconds to a minute when a lot of mental activity will be going on. I have difficulty waiting because my "voices" say everyone is bored and falling asleep. From consistent feedback that I didn't wait long enough, I have learned to have patience. The first paragraph includes guidance in relaxing. See Appendix II for more instructions on how to relax.

The Lead Vault And Iron Door

Take three deep breaths, pulling in life energy as you inhale and releasing tension and stress on the exhale.

Imagine you are walking down a path, and you see a vault . . . a large, thick, old iron and lead vault with many locks on it . . . Walk up to it . . . As you come close you realize that inside are those things you don't want to see just yet . . . Walk up to it anyway . . . What are you feeling? . . . Unlock the locks . . . pull the door open . . . What are you feeling? . . . Take your flashlight and shine it inside, shed some light on what you will find . . . What do you see? . . . What are the colors? . . . What is the air like? . . . Smells? . . . What do you feel? . . . When you are ready, leave the vault . . . Shut the door if you would like. Bring your attention back here.

Move up out of your body and look back down on this room of people . . . How do they look? . . . How do you feel? . . .

Now return to your body to stay. When you are ready, open
your eyes and join us back here.

People have many different reactions to this imagery depending on the issues they are preparing to face. Clients have described seeing snakes, breasts, penises and a treasure chest. The
treasure chest was seen by a woman who had been uncomfortable with her sexuality and used many ways to avoid knowing
she was having sex. She discovered from taking a class that it
was possible to enjoy her sexuality, and this was represented by
a treasure chest full of delights to explore. Some people don't see
a clear image, but have a thought when they look in. Others
hear something significant. In the group we talk about the things
people saw, assuming that what they imagine is either an actual
event they need to remember or a symbol of it.

Imagery can be used as a way to tell your story. I often tell
people to "make it up," knowing they are only making up the
details while the essence of what they tell is true. Make your
story as wild and absurd as you want to, and wait until you are
done to see what you might have revealed to yourself.

Our Dreams Speak To Us

Several times during the night our unconscious creates a
story for us to watch or take part in. Dreams are one of the
ways we can collect information about what is going on in our
unconscious so we can bring memories out of repression and
change their impact on our lives. As you know, our unconscious
tries to grab them back in the morning to keep us from finding
out the truth. Sometimes we are left with strong feelings from
a dream that has gone back into the recesses of repressed memories, often without remembering the dream itself. Sometimes
a small amount of the dream remains but the story is lost. We
can use these pieces.

If you remember a whole dream, writing it down will retain
it for you even when your unconscious wipes it out. Recording
and analyzing your dreams is the subject of a book called *Dream
Power* by Anne Faraday. She has wonderful methods for milking
your dreams of all kinds of information, from remembering
what you need to do that day to expressing anger that went
underground.

A dream fragment or just a feeling can also be used. I make up dreams from either one, and the effect is the same as telling a dream that I can remember. Information that is unclear and seems to be fed to me in indirect ways falls into place as I utter the words.

Retelling dreams is a useful way to create change in your perceptions. I often launch into telling my dream the way I wanted it to go with full emotion as if I were a powerful story-teller. I began this practice one morning when I woke up feeling powerless and useless. I had dreamed that my wedding to Rex was about to take place and there was some confusion about which woman he should marry. The mother of a woman he had been engaged to some years before stood up in the chapel and said that he didn't want to marry me, he was going to marry her daughter. Rex wasn't around to ask about this. I went immediately into a submissive, fearful stance, assuming if she said this was so then it was.

I woke up feeling depressed and lifeless, the victim of my environment. As I began to tell Rex the dream, I realized that I hated that feeling and wasn't willing to have the dream go that way. I sat up in bed, with my arms out and my voice strong, and I told him that I had walked to the altar, turned and pointed to the mother and cried out, "You will be shot at dawn!" I felt wonderfully strong and had an energized day even without interpreting the meanings of the dream. I have become a passionate storyteller as I retell the ones that pull me into less than full living.

Writing "Fictional" Stories

When all else fails to provide information, the fictional story always works for me. If you like to write, this method can be useful. The instructions are simple. Sit down with your keyboard or pen and begin.

Start with a subject you are interested in learning more about, such as what happened when you were a small child or your real feelings about the person you are in a relationship with. Feelings that seem to land on you without explanation are also a good subject. When you have experienced what it is you want to write about, then put it out of your mind. Sit down with a blank mind and free-associate.

Let whatever comes flow out of your fingers with the censor turned off. If you think about punctuation or sentence structure you will lose the value of the exercise. Don't go back and correct anything — you could lose important data.

If a title enters your thoughts, write it down without trying to understand it. If one doesn't and you are having a hard time getting started, begin with "Once upon a time . . ." and see what follows. You could also add, ". . . a little girl/boy . . ." Write in the third person, as if you were creating a story about another person entirely. "This little girl climbed up the steps to the front door, wondering what it would be like in there. Yearning for safety, she . . ." You will feel as if you are writing about someone else, but of course it is yourself.

During the writing process you must suspend evaluation and interpretation. If you don't, your unconscious will shut down the information you are permitting it to reveal. The task is to act as if you are just writing "fiction" so the truth will come out. We can make use of the fact that our unconscious wants desperately to express what is going on. But this communication about what occurred years ago has to be out of our conscious awareness so we can obey the rule, "Thou Shalt Not Be Aware." We offer our unconscious the opportunity to speak by disguising what is revealed.

Write the story until it is finished and then stop, whether you have one paragraph or five pages. Now comes the interpretation. Take your story and go to another part of the room. Look at the paper in your hand as if it were written by someone else, and begin reading. If any feelings come up, let them flow out. Your unconscious gatekeeper may not allow you to feel what you have written. If so, two more steps can help. Read your story to a recovering friend. Then have your friend read it to you. Listen as if the story were about someone else.

Videotape Your Story And Be Your Own Audience

I have a video camera in my office that I often leave on during a session. If something happens that I would like to show my client, I can rewind and play it on the monitor. I discovered that when we listen to our story as if someone else were telling it we are able to have the compassion and belief that we cannot extend to ourselves. I have seen people criticize themselves while telling their story and then cry compassionately when watching the same story on the monitor. If you have access to a video camera you can record your story and then listen back. It can be more effective to wait a day or so to review it. Your group might spend a meeting or two taping each person's story, renting the camera if necessary. The stories can be played back and digested over the next few meetings.

What If Someone's Story Is Arousing?

Great! You have more information about your own cross-wiring. As the sexual arousal emerges, check back to what the person was talking about when your reaction began. There is something similar of importance in your own background, and this similarity triggered your physiological reaction. This is the same as feeling sad when someone else is feeling sad. It is your own sadness you feel, not the speaker's. When you have done all your own crying, then when others are sad they won't trigger your sadness. Instead, you might feel delighted that they are discharging their feelings.

Not long ago I was standing on the platform that extends out over a very long drop into the water beneath Snoqualmie Falls near Seattle, when I became aware that I had a strong sexual sensation in my genitals. In the past I had ignored this feeling, but this time I examined it. I walked up to the edge and looked down, finding the arousal becoming more intense. As I walked away and was less frightened, the arousal lessened. I breathed deeply and opened myself to any connections that might come.

I remembered sitting on my father's shoulders and being terrified of the height and chagrined that I couldn't do what my siblings seemed to enjoy. I can guess that being held in ways that felt unsafe became associated with arousal during the sexual stimulation I received in my very early years. I didn't learn any more about the connections. The next time the association comes up, I will be aware more quickly and can continue the exploration.

12

Unlearning
The Rules Of
Sexual Functioning

Cultural rules about sexuality dominate our sexual activity
— even though no one has ever mentioned them to us. We can
examine and relinquish each rule so we can discover spontaneous, inside-out sexual energy. Once we can talk openly about
sex, have access to feelings and have begun the unwiring process, we can examine all training from both family of origin and
our culture. Then we can decide which rules of sexual functioning to eliminate.

An effective way to begin is to *change your focus when you are*
having sex from the sex itself to the rules that dominate sexual activity.
The rule that says Thou Shalt Not Be Aware is so deeply
ingrained, however, that most people find it difficult to see we
are operating by rules. Setting a timer to go off every ten
minutes can help. When it rings, you and your partner can
check to see whether you are following rules and speak them
to each other.

Rex and I began this process the first time we had sex, and we continue to use it. As we cleared out the first large wave of interfering rules, we found that their numbers diminished to only one or two at a time. Each time we are ready to move to a new level of intimacy we run up against a new rule that hadn't been conscious before. The cleaning process is a long, fascinating one.

I would like to tell you about the first time we got into bed after having decided to change our relationship from a loving friendship to a sexual one. We weren't driven by strong sexual attraction and actually had no outside-in attraction for each other. Neither of us looked "right" by the other's cross-wired definition of a sexually attractive person, primarily because I am taller than he is. This allowed us to explore our friendship with no thought about its becoming sexual — a wonderful experience that our cross-wiring had prohibited in our other relationships. Once we realized we were delightful companions, it seemed obvious that sex should be part of the picture. The decision was based on logic rather than lust.

Already free of lust and arousal based on external attributes, we could relatively calmly take off our clothes and bring our bodies together. As we touched and smiled at each other, our arousal came up and we moved into sexual activity. Then Rex's erection went down. His first reaction was to work on increasing his arousal so it would come back up. I had been working on my sexuality for some time, so I had the objectivity to know this approach wouldn't enhance our lovemaking. I didn't go along with trying to retrieve his erection. Instead I just acknowledged that his penis was down and continued to hug him. This was the first contradiction to his belief that he had to have an erection when being sexual and must do anything to regain it if it dropped. He was shocked and delighted, and he quickly began to reexamine his patterned way of responding.

As his penis went up and down that night, he grew less critical and more curious about the reasons. Each time it went down he reflected on what was going on inside and came upon a variety of cross-wired beliefs by letting his "inner voices" speak. One was that if he got too wild and carried away he might hurt me. A second was that he "shouldn't" enjoy himself this much and it was time to stop.

A third voice said, "You better not lose this erection or you won't be a real man," which brought up performance fear, which in turn reduced his sexual arousal. After years of this performance issue, he had come to anticipate that he would lose his erection and feel shame about it. Every time he had sex he began with the expectation that he would lose his erection, and this fear brought it about. The continued contradiction of Rex's old voices quieted them in short order and the patterned reasons for loss of erection entirely disappeared.

There is another reason his erection goes down, but it is not based on rules. Sometimes we have had sex when it really isn't the right time. We may have some leftover feelings from a disagreement, one of us needs to sleep or his mind is focused away from the relationship for a time. He learned to respect these reasons for loss of erection and merely acknowledge their existence. This hasn't occurred for a long time because we have trained our "sniffers" to alert us to these variables, so we don't get started with sexual activity if there are reasons not to. On the contrary, almost all the time that one of us feels sexual the other does as well.

We discovered another set of patterned reactions as our relationship developed. The intensity of a new love relationship and our awareness that we were becoming life partners swept us along in our sexual interest for one another. We always had sex when we got together, sometimes two or three times a day. We believed it would always be like that because it was so pleasurable. But it didn't last. We reached the point where we were satisfied going for days without sex when we didn't seem to have anything unresolved that kept us from it. The days would occasionally stretch into weeks.

When this change in frequency began I had wild voices yelling at me. They said I had to have sex and I was causing this unfair situation to occur, much as I had in my first marriage. I feared it was happening again, even though none of the negatives of that marriage existed in this one. When we were cuddling and feeling sexual I pushed myself to sexual activity, "trying" to get more aroused. I apologized to him if I couldn't manage to overcome the physical barriers or the emotional ones.

After a time I began to examine this more closely. I acknowledged to myself that I didn't understand what was happening because things weren't the way I had predicted they would be. So I decided to pay attention to the feelings that came up when I was reluctant to have sex. I allowed the voices to speak, with Rex's permission. They said things such as, *"No, no, no,* I'm not

going to do it," and, "You're going to leave me if I don't take care
of your sexual needs." As soon as the words were out of my
mouth I laughed and then Rex laughed as we saw the absurdity.
I soon was able to *not be sexual* often enough to really believe I
had no responsibility to take care of "my man's" "sexual needs."
That pattern died.

As I gave myself permission to be exactly the way I was, I
began to notice that Rex was no more interested than I was. I
had made up the idea that he wanted sex when we were aroused
and that he expected me to perform. It turned out that when
we didn't have sex, neither of us were wanting it. And when we
did want sex, both of us wanted it.

Rex's patterns then came into focus. He believed that as a man
he should always want sex, so it was hard for him to know that
when I didn't want sex, he didn't either. His male socialization
says that he mustn't go for a week without sex and feel fine
about it. If he is a real man he will object to my lack of interest
and want me to want sex more. Once my patterns fell away,
then he had to become conscious of his. He who had rarely gone
a day without an orgasm was content to go a week or sometimes
several weeks without one. I remember the smile on his face and
his little laugh when he realized he no longer had to subscribe to
the rules about being a real man. He could cherish his sexual
energy and use it only when it was right for him and for us.

Following these changes we found it quite easy to let go of
the remnants of the rule that you must have sex if you are in a
relationship. As these last particles faded away we were left
with real permission to use sexual energy in ways that opened
us to each other and bonded us deeply. We found that when
either of us was highly involved in our creativity or work projects, we didn't want to have sex because it would pull our
attention away. Then when we were both looking toward each
other again, we would find ourselves having sex — when the
time was right. Long, luxurious, melting sex. We would focus
all of our attention into our bonding. Sex became a creative
process, much as writing is for me and sculpture is for Rex. In
all such activities we have to allow our complete attention to
flow into our creations. If we need to be doing something else
the full creation cannot occur.

I believe initially we need to make love with sex to form a new
family coupling. Sexual energy speeds up the process by demanding our full attention, inviting us to spend great amounts of time

together and explore each other deeply. When we complete this process, then sexual creation no longer dominates the relationship and takes its turn along with other interests. As our interest turns again to each other we rebond with sexual energy.

Before we met, Rex and I had both worked on our addictive sexuality for a time (although we didn't call it that because neither of us had heard it named back then). I was aware that I had been triangulated into my parent's relationship, but not that I had been sexually touched. Rex had no idea he was the victim of childhood incest. As our sexual loving was settling into a comfortable part of our lives, new levels of information emerged. Rex retrieved his first memory of a sexual contact that occurred when he was about three. I became aware of my first body memory of sexual abuse when he was Rolfing me. We knew these experiences must be influencing our sexual exchanges, particularly since we no longer engaged in rule-dominated or addictive sexual activities. We were more open to these new issues being expressed in sex.

We can assume that our histories of incest influenced our sex all along, but it was only now they could become visible. We both feared the power of sex, expressing it as a belief that we would become one and shoot off into the stratosphere, never to be seen again. It sounded funny when we said it, but no other images came up. We think our childhood sexual experiences led us to believe sex was powerful and dangerous, to be used only when carefully contained by rules. When I imagine the experience of a child being aroused while being used sexually, I believe the situation would seem dangerous and out of control. A child doesn't have the emotional and mental maturity to comprehend adult sexuality and is truly a victim of its power.

As Rex and I cleaned away all the distractors and the overriding need to bond, these old terrors were free to come up. Our tasks now are to respect every scrap of fear that arises when we are being sexual and to let the fear tell its story. We have a powerful door to our childhoods as we learn how to understand our adult sexual experience.

Cultural Rules About Sex

I have listed some of the rules that our culture imposes and reinforces in our families of origin. These may come up as you take a look at your sexual activity.

1. *Couples must have sex.* This rule must be broken to make way for breaking the rest.
2. *Sex starts with kissing.* On the contrary, sex can start with intercourse or anywhere else both people want.
3. *Sex ends with the man's orgasm.* Orgasms are not necessary to a completed sex act.
4. *Everything between the kiss and the orgasm is predictable.* "Sex by numbers" is over. Those pushy rules will try to tell you that you *must* go to another activity *now*, but instead you can flow into it from your intuition.
5. *Good lovers focus on the other person.* Wonderful sex can focus on the self, and other wonderful sex focuses on the couple with lots of eye contact.
6. *High arousal is important to attain.* Arousal is a signal to proceed and the absence of it says "not now." That's all. It's also a powerful tool for loving. But you can't *make* arousal happen naturally, you can only *let* it happen.
7. *If the man loses his erection it means there is a problem.* It means he has lost his erection. That's all.
8. *If the woman loses her arousal it means he isn't a good lover or there is something wrong with her.* She has just lost her arousal.
9. *If a couple "only" caress and arouse gentle sexual energy they have not had sex.* A complete sexual act can take place with a deep kiss. We haven't had sex if "it" doesn't "go in." We are virgins until it goes in. Adultery doesn't occur if there is no penis/vagina penetration. Changing the definition of sex changes the number of lovers we have had.
10. *A man can "take" a woman but a woman cannot "take" a man.* Letting go of this rule allows the woman to make love spontaneously to the man and sometimes control the lovemaking, and it allows him to surrender himself to her.
11. *The man is responsible for the woman's orgasm.* A man cannot make love to a woman's body if he focuses on doing it "right." If both believe there is no responsibility for an outcome, then he is free to really get to know her body and she is free to get to know his.
12. *Sexual arousal must "go somewhere" — it is not an end in itself.* Each level of arousal is an end in itself, and it may or may not go somewhere else.
13. *Other.* Add your own.

New Guidelines

As you shift your attention in sex to these interfering rules, some new guidelines can help until the process becomes more automatic.

1. *Let the rules speak every time you are aware they are speaking.* If you find your arousal dropping tell your partner. Then let the voices speak out loud. For example, they may say, "I must make myself get aroused again" or "Something's wrong with me" or "Oh, no, I'm failing and I'm not a good lover."
2. *Put sexual activity second to communicating thoughts and feelings.* If either of you feels sex must continue, then it becomes impossible to stop at any moment to learn how the rules are dominating your loving.
3. *Discuss your sexual activity after it feels complete.* In the process of learning to recognize rules most of them will go by you unseen. Replaying your sexual interaction aloud can allow more information to surface for you to work on. This will also help you be more conscious the next time the rule appears.

My good friend Karen has been working for some time on her disinclination to have sex with her husband, whom she dearly loves and with whom she shares a lifetime commitment. Karen and Jack believed she had some "problems" that prevented her from wanting to have sex with him. They had sought sex therapy more than ten years ago and had done a long series of exercises, but nothing changed. Jack waited for her to improve. Karen kept working on it.

Things did not begin to change until Karen was able to tell Jack she would no longer agree that sex was part of their marriage contract and she no longer wanted to have sex. At the same time she began RC co-counseling sessions on her early sexual memories and did other kinds of therapeutic activities that would allow her to make sense of what was happening. As she took charge of her sexuality and refused to obey cultural edicts, she began to feel the power of knowing she was entitled to a satisfying, healthy sex life.

Now focused on creating her own sexual health, she moved toward her sexual healing instead of feeling pressured to change in order to meet her marital requirements. Soon after this she attended an RC Early Sexual Memories workshop and experienced the first memories of a sexually abusive relationship with her father when she was very young. Her idealization of him had made it impossible for her to think he had used her sexually.

As Karen recovered these memories, she had a dream that her husband was really like her father. As she worked on the dream the common elements emerged. Her father made her his sex object, using her for his gratification. She was to focus on his needs rather than hers. His exuding of sexual energy in order to appear to be a bright, charismatic man was his attempt to be cared about through his sexuality.

As Karen became aware of her father's attributes, she could see how her husband's were similar even though on the surface the two men were not at all the same. Jack approached her as a sex object because he carried such intense feelings of shame about his own sexuality that he couldn't remain conscious when being sexual. She described his body as becoming rigid and hard when he became aroused. She seemed to disappear from his vision. His desire for sex seemed to be more a need for a guarantee of love, and for that reason she felt dishonest when having sex. Karen had felt required by him, herself and her sex therapists to focus on Jack's needs for her to be sexual with him. It was a replay of the childhood situation where her father's needs came first.

Once Karen became aware of these similarities she was in a very different position to work with her sexuality. She was now able to differentiate between several patterns that prevented her from wanting to be sexual with Jack. She could also make very real choices about when it was right for her to be sexual. She no longer saw herself as the "identified patient" who was causing the sexual problems. It was clear that her patterns were responding to Jack's patterns. She was now in a position to point out to Jack what was happening on his side that would also prevent them from having sex.

Karen explained to Jack that she would not ever be interested in having sex with him when he became a rigid board. She would not use her sexuality to focus on his "needs" or to reassure him that he was loved.

Jack was startled but able to take in what Karen had said. He had been attending the RC Early Sexual Memories support group with Karen and was working intensely on the shaming of his sexuality that occurred in his childhood. As his shame dropped, his understanding of his sexuality became clear. Until Karen told him what she learned, he had no reason to suspect that her disinclination had anything to do with him. Once he had the information, he could examine his own sexual history and work on patterns that were preventing him from using sex in a loving, bonding, unfolding way. He could influence his sex life with Karen instead of sitting helplessly by waiting for her to change.

13

Creating A
Support Group

We who are recovering from addictiveness are setting out in
increasing numbers to remove the influences of our culture and
free ourselves from the constraints of the addictive process.
The proliferation of 12-Step programs, beginning with Alcoholics Anonymous, demonstrates the need for people gathering
together to create a new sub-culture that dares to violate the
rules of the old dominant culture. Alcoholics Anonymous was
followed by Narcotics Anonymous, and Al-Anon was created
for the families of addicts. More recently programs for sex
addicts, adult children and other groups of people who want to
use the 12-Step program to heal have been started. CODA,
which stands for Co-dependents Anonymous, has come into
being and is growing rapidly. When well-known speakers in
these fields give lectures in large areas, they have audiences in
the thousands.

We are *talking* now. We are telling family secrets and refusing to go along with the old "dysfunctional family" ways. We are hearing each other's stories and seeing that the world is not the mythical portrayals of our families and other authorities. When we see what is under the surface we can begin to change the rules that say "don't feel," "struggle hard to get ahead," "everyone is monogamous," "sex isn't to be talked about," "you are sick if you have strong feelings of any sort but something is wrong with you if you don't have sympathy and compassion for the less fortunate," "have a drink to unwind and champagne to celebrate," etc.

Twelve-Step meetings offer an opportunity for experience that I believe is unequalled anywhere else. There people reach out to anyone who wants to talk about his or her pain and learn how to heal from it. Twelve-Step programs reflect the pervasiveness of our culture's dysfunction and then help to diminish it. When ten or 80 or 300 people gather in a room to share their commitment to recovery, it is truly powerful. When we can go to almost any community in our country and find a gathering of program people who will welcome us, it speaks to the force of this movement. The programs are not advertised, no one sets out to sign anyone up and there is no marketing program. Yet millions of people attend meetings on a regular basis and are experiencing vast life changes. The word spreads from person to person. This process gathers strength as the community expands and creates a new culture that allows us to abandon the old one with its dysfunctional ways.

Talking and showing who we really are, with the safety of anonymity, is essential to changing the old culture. We have repressed our memories and shoved our awareness of our true selves out of consciousness. We have done this to obey the rules of our families and culture. The only way to retrieve our real self and see the dysfunctional rules we are following is to *talk* and to *listen to the stories of others*. These two actions, along with experiencing our feelings, will allow our unconscious awarenesses to surface. We must have an accurate mirror for this to happen.

I encourage you to join this major movement that is creating a cultural shift. If you don't qualify for Sex Addicts Anonymous, Alcoholics Anonymous or other substance-based programs, you may join Co-dependents Anonymous (CODA). Because we live in a co-dependent culture that has contaminated us, we are all co-dependent.

Twelve-Step groups for sexual issues exist in most large communities and are discussed in Chapter 9. If your community doesn't have such a group, you might consider forming your own. You can receive help with this process by writing to the centers listed in Chapter 9, or asking your local Alcoholics Anonymous. In addition to participating in a 12-Step group you may want to create a support group to talk about the forbidden subject of sex. This chapter presents one way to create such a group.

Talking About Sexuality

We have remained silent our entire life about our sexuality and sexual upbringing. To learn about them requires talking about our sexual self and listening to other people's stories. To do this on our own with unrecovering people is to meet with all the objections and cultural rules that have kept us silent for so long. Exposing ourselves to such reactions makes it likely that we will return to silence because social sanctions are powerful. The alternative is to gather people together and establish a safe environment to learn about sexuality by talking about it and to discharge feelings.

Members of support or study groups must agree to specific boundaries at the outset because sex is such a volatile subject. Because most of the group will *not* have a clear understanding of sexual boundaries, rules for all will create individual safety that does not yet come from within.

Setting Up A Support Group

Ground Rules

The following five rules can provide some safety while investigating your sexual story. Your group may decide to add to or modify them.

1. *No sexual energy expressed between group members* unless they are already in a sexual relationship. This requirement is extremely important in order to provide safety from the hidden

social and personal rules that dominate sexual activity and relating. You can assume that any sexual energy arising between group members is cross-wired, so it should be the object of examination rather than action. Engaging sexual energy from "innocent" flirting to having sex will damage the group, prohibit safety and lead to the dissolution of the group.

Members of our culture may not know when we are engaging sexual energy. This is important feedback to give group members so they can learn from it. We can give this feedback in non-shaming ways.

2. *Everything is confidential.* The agreement among members to keep confidential everything that goes on in the room is necessary for you to open up to unfamiliar parts of yourself. You may choose later to reveal everything you have said, but you will have the safety of knowing that it's your decision.

3. *Attendance at meetings is a commitment.* You will want to know you are interacting with other people who will be there consistently and are as involved as you are in this process. Members of the group need to commit to attending meetings whenever possible so each person can expect this from the others.

4. *Do not form friendships or lover relationships* with group members you did not know before the group began. A clear division between your friendships and your support group relationships provides safety. When a friendship develops you can experience confusion that interferes with using the support well. Friendships require a lot of work beyond what the support group requires. For a variety of reasons, feelings will come up that must be addressed. This ground rule avoids the creation of extra feelings and thus provides safety as you focus exclusively on your sexual story-telling. Honor the importance of your task by creating a group that is as free as possible of extraneous factors.

5. *Do not use alcohol or other drugs* before or during gatherings. They prevent the flow of real feelings and will interfere with your process and disrupt the experience of others in the group.

Number Of People

Different size groups offer different values to members. The minimum is three people and there is no maximum. Six to eight is a manageable sized group in which all people will get their turn to talk. Larger groups provide the opportunity to experience a whole new community of people doing what you are doing, and they usually provide safety while you are abandoning some strict social rules. If your group grows into a large one, you can also divide up into smaller units for the benefit of being heard as you tell your story. This can be done by meeting as a whole for a period, and deciding how many subgroups are desired for the remainder of the meeting time. If you decide you want four subgroups this can be done by counting off by fours. All the "ones" gather together, the "twos" together, etc.

Dividing Time

In most 12-Step meetings the leader opens the meeting for sharing, giving each person an opportunity to speak if they wish. People who are doing formal RC divide the time evenly, setting a timer so it is clear when each person's turn begins and ends. This works particularly well because it disengages our co-dependent patterns of wanting to be sure we aren't taking too much time and resenting it if someone takes more than a fair share.

I experience a powerful impact from knowing I have three minutes (or five minutes or 15 minutes) in which to take something from inside of me and put it outside. I have discovered I am capable of telling something completely and discharging a great amount of emotion in a very short period of time. If I had an hour I would take an hour, but if I only have seven minutes I can still do it.

Meeting Between Group Meetings

Most people find that telling their story is more powerful and valuable in a group of several people. There is something about seeing many eyes looking with acceptance that reaches into the core of a person. However, in a group of seven or more people your time will be limited to 10 or 15 minutes. It is also valuable to be able to talk for half an hour or an hour with good attention from others. This need can be met by getting together with two other people between group sessions for one to two hours and dividing the time. Make specific appointments that include both the starting time and the length of the meeting.

It is particularly important to meet with *two other people* or more to avoid the possibility of reenacting an abusive situation from your childhood. *Please don't assume there weren't any.* All of us were sexually abused in some fashion, if only through the shame we picked up from our parents when they saw evidence of our sexuality.

When I was participating in RC activities in Alaska, we met at each other's homes for both the large and small groups. Classes were held in homes or sometimes in a therapy group room. Public places such as restaurants are not conducive to the open discharge of feeling that is so beneficial.

How To Listen

The following guidelines provide a structure of safety to break the no-talk rules. These are time-tested and work well.

1. You get your turn.
2. Listen with loving attention.
3. No cross-talking.
4. No interpreting.
5. No "active listening" or paraphrasing.
6. Speak little and only when you are clear it can be helpful.

When you are talking about sexual things and feeling the many feelings that come up, you need other people in the room to listen with their full attention. Given that this is the agreement of the group and you know you have the full time set on the timer, you are free to talk without having your attention drawn to the needs of others. Yours are the only needs addressed during your time. Each person in turn becomes the center of attention.

As you are talking it can be helpful to focus directly on one person from the group (or from your triad when you meet with only two other people). You can ask this person to touch you and decide how far or close he or she should be from you. Physical contact such as holding hands, a hand on your back or an arm around you can increase your feelings of safety. For others safety comes from knowing there will be no contact. Check with yourself to see what you want.

This is your time. You are the one who gets to talk or even to sit silently with group attention. You get to experience taking your time to say what you want and being free of interruption by others. Normally in social interaction the conversation flows back and forth between group members with no structure. This "cross talking" inhibits individual talking in support groups.

Interpreting meanings or giving advice also interferes with the purpose of support groups. Attention is pulled to the interpretation or advice and away from the basic experience of talking.

"Active listening," or paraphrasing what the speaker has said, is a very useful tool for learning how to communicate effectively but is not useful here. Support groups for the purpose of talking about the unmentionable and having feelings are not about communication. It doesn't matter if others don't understand what you say. It only matters that they listen with good attention.

When you are the listener there are *rare* times when speaking one sentence is helpful. More than one sentence will distract the person from the process in which they are engaged. Some possible one-liners are:

"You can take your time" or "You have plenty of time." This can be useful if a person is rushing through the story and not allowing feelings to flow along with the words. I find this reminder helpful when I am telling something that is still hard to talk about. My body becomes stiff, I stop breathing fully and I feel I am pushing the words out. If a group member tells me I can take my time, my body relaxes as I remember I don't *have* to tell it. I take a deep breath and pay attention to the feelings instead of the words.

"It's okay to feel it." This can give permission to contradict the belief that having feelings will result in something terrible.

Sometimes repeating back a key sentence will help a person feel what they have just said. When we talk about something that is coming out of repression, it can feel as if we are making it up or haven't really said it. Hearing someone else say a sentence back can allow us to "see" it more clearly ourselves. For example, the first time I told that I had been sexual with my little sister when I was three, it sounded like something no one would believe. When my listener said, "You were sexual with your sister," it suddenly sounded real.

As your group gets underway, you can try out different kinds of one-liners to see what is effective. Some will be and others won't. But remember to use them sparingly.

14

Increasing Awareness: Letting Our Body Speak

We have been trained over a lifetime to ignore what is going on in our body. Sexuality is suppressed by shaming any signs of it and shaming the body, followed by the commandment "Thou Shalt Not Be Aware." Our culture's pressure to suppress feelings has deprived us of receiving information from our body about its needs and pleasures. We had to overlook this information in order to ignore emerging feelings asking for expression. Now that we are ready to reclaim our healthy sexual energy, it is time to reclaim awareness of our body.

Remembering

We remember in many ways. Pictures and thoughts that appear in our mind are only one form of memory although our culture teaches us this is the only valid one. Body memory is seen as "just" sensations in the body.

One way we remember, vital to understanding our cross-wiring, is through our bodies. Everything that has happened to us physically has been recorded in our cells and is waiting to be remembered once we know how to receive and decode the bodily information. Our bodies tell the story of our childhood abuses in the same way our behavior does: We reenact the story.

The repositioning of fat deposits, pelvis and other body parts, as I described in Chapter 6, communicates something about what happened in sexual and non-sexual ways. As I've mentioned, physical symptoms, such as a chronically tight throat, holding tension in certain body parts and feelings of skin irritation can be our body speaking about the past. "Holding patterns" and different texture in the tissue can inform knowledgeable body workers about areas that are carrying memories of something that didn't go right. Feelings of revulsion or of sexual arousal from a particular kind of touch can result from a body memory. Even if no obvious abuse was occurring when someone touched us, *our body even remembers the person's intent*. The rule "Thou Shalt Not Be Aware" has deprived us of knowing how to learn from our bodies what is wrong and what to do about it. The direct route to relearning how to listen to our physical selves is to *attend to our bodies in new ways*.

Increasing Awareness

Stimulation of our bodies can bring back awareness when we are ready to know what it remembers. There are many non-threatening, non-sexual ways to stimulate ourselves physically. This chapter will describe some of them. You may use these to supplement what you may already be doing.

Exercise

Any regular exercise is a good start, and the more muscles you use the better. As you run or swim or walk pay attention to your physical self. Headphones or thinking about other things will deprive you of listening to your body's instructions about what it needs and wants. If you do aerobic exercise, *let your body tell you what to do* next and how fast. Do not feel constrained to obey an instructor. A good stretching program is a powerful way to rediscover your physical being, but only if you guide it yourself, allowing your body to tell you what it needs and staying with a stretch as long as it continues to feel good. Instructors can teach you how to do stretches and exercises until you have reached the point where you can learn from your body. If you have shut off your awareness, a good teacher will know more about your body than you do. As you become aware, then a person on the outside can give you information but cannot know all of what your body is able to tell you.

Breathing

Attending to how you are breathing serves several functions. First, it brings awareness to your body. Second, when you think about breathing you are likely to breathe more deeply, increasing consciousness of your body. Third, by paying attention you will see what is amiss and begin correcting it.

> Stop for a moment and attend to your breathing. Observe it without trying to change it. Is it shallow or deep? Tight or relaxed? How much of your lung capacity are you using? Do you breathe in your chest or abdomen or both? Spend two minutes or more seeing what happens when you pay attention.
>
> Now go back to Chapter 10 and do the Breathing Practice Exercise. When you finish, pay attention to what happens to your breathing. Has anything changed? Attend now to your feelings. Are you feeling any more? And last, attend to your awareness of what is happening in your body. Where does your attention focus? What might that part of your body be trying to tell you?

Quiet Time

We live in a culture that stimulates our senses, and this outside-in stimulation prevents us from attending to the gentle messages that come constantly from inside. We can allow the soft messages to be heard by quieting down the outside stimulus that overpowers them. We can build quiet hours, peaceful vacations and calm weekends into the plan of our lives. When we must be in distracting situations, it is often possible to reduce some of the intensity. For example, when choosing a restaurant or a grocery store see which ones stimulate you with sound, light and hustle. Find those that allow you to focus on yourself, taste your dinner and select foods that are right for you. Avoid those places where you tense up. For example, a mall in Seattle is filled with neon, loud music and startling people. Even though

I may want to buy things available there, I avoid this mall except for short excursions because it "revs" me up and distracts me from myself. If I go to a mall during its slow hours I find the tension created by masses of people greatly reduced.

The more time I spend in solitude the more I find myself automatically attending to the messages from inside. I know when I am hungry and for what food and I know when I need sleep, as well as countless other bodily preferences. The more I access this inside information, the less I am willing to be perpetually stimulated from outside.

Hydrotherapy

Saunas, steam baths and whirlpools increase our awareness of our physical self. Becoming very hot and then applying cold water in a shower or pool (alternating heat and cold two to three times, ending with cold) will cleanse your body deeply and allow you new relaxation. If you haven't done this before, it might feel like torture the first time or two. But once your body sees how wonderful it is, it becomes pleasurable to heat up and then apply cold water. Your body is the source of information about how long to heat and how best to cool.

Hot springs or warm springs provide the added beneficial effect of minerals in the water. Many resorts that have been built around the springs also offer massage; the two can be a powerful combination.

Body Boundaries

I have experimented with different approaches to body awareness and have selected those that seem useful. I suggest you do the same, using as many as you can. Those I discuss here are only some of the many kinds of bodywork and movement work.

As I tried different approaches I discovered an important principle. *The qualities of the person touching me are far more important than the discipline she or he practices.* I have had the finest Rolfing by a gifted woman whose skill goes far beyond her training (Marita Bott who practices in Hawaii), and I have experienced violation of boundaries, physical abuse and sexualization of a professional relationship by a Rolfer. One massage therapist (Kathryn Maxwell, who now practices Naturopathic Medicine in Seattle) puts a hand on my body and knows exactly where to go next to free me of blocks I am struggling with. I experience her "knowing" me and my body trusts her. The five Trager practitioners I have experienced were all in tune with my body, but one stands out as having excellent clarity about both of our boundaries (Nancy Bonifield, Seattle). A massage therapist at Breitenbush Hot Springs in Oregon (Willow) was safe to be with because she was acutely present with me. I could trust she wouldn't violate my body.

Of the more than 20 bodyworkers I have seen, at least half were good at their work and I would return to them. I felt violated by four. I didn't stay for a session with one person because *I wasn't "seen"* at all. A "procedure" was about to be done *to* me.

When I was violated by my first Rolfer in 1975, I had no idea I had a right to sensitive care with boundaries. I went to him for a "treatment" and I thought I *had to receive it* as if it were medical. He left me with bruises, expected I would "deal with" the pain and he sexualized our relating. As I stood in front of him in my bathing suit so he could decide what needed correcting, he told me I was a sexy woman. I felt immensely uncomfortable. Since I didn't feel sexy, I thought he was lying to me to make me feel good. At that time I thought this "technique" must be appropriate and any discomfort I felt was due to my issues. Part of me knew, however, that this was wrong for me. I didn't go to another Rolfer to finish the series, and I deliberately directed people away from Rolfing until I met Rex. Even when it was clear that human-inflicted pain was not healthy for me, I still didn't know that the sexual energy he employed also severely violated our relationship and me.

After Rex and I had known each other for several months I resumed Rolfing. By this time in my life I knew I wouldn't tolerate pain or sexualizing, yet I was still frightened when I arrived at Rex's office for my appointment. After a session in which I felt no sexual energy and a true connection between us, I could see that the procedure done to me many years before was more akin to torture than care of my body. I am delighted to know that Rolfing is powerful work without the need for pain.

Don't stay with a bodyworker who is abusing you in even the smallest ways. The effect is to recreate the abuse you received as a child. If you are uncomfortable with a person before you even get on the table you can leave without paying. If the session seems tolerable but afterward you realize you aren't interested in continuing with this person, don't go back. Try someone else.

More and more bodyworkers are sensitive to sexual and physical abuse issues and the effects on the body. You can interview people about how they handle these issues and select someone who is willing to back off when you aren't comfortable. You must be in control of what happens to your body to remove the effects of the mishandling you received as a child. In *For Your Own Good*, Alice Miller describes how our culture abuses children in ways that are supposed to help. The child is expected to accept the rationalization that it is good for him or her. Healing from this cultural influence requires saying *no*, and *take your hands off me* and *don't touch me like that*. Even when you know it is "for your own good" you can say *NO, NO, NO*.

Below are some forms of bodywork you can explore as you retrieve awareness of your body and its communications to you.

Rolfing

Rolfing has been effective for me and for my clients as we retrieve our sense of Self. Through extensive discussion with Rex and observation of the effects on my clients, I have come to see the powerful benefits of Rolfing. I highly recommend the ten-session series to anyone who wants to encourage emotional, psychological or physical unfolding. Rolfing is advertised as a form of bodywork that corrects posture, allows more comfort in the body, reduces some forms of chronic pain and can help athletic performance. I am most interested in the psychological benefits created by the disruption of old, staid patterns. As the body is physically realigned the old patterns are interrupted, including the pattern of not being aware.

Rolfing works on the fascia, which is connective tissue in the body. Rex describes it as a fibrous packing material that gives our bodies shape, as well as ligaments, tendons and scar tissue. Rolfers manipulate this tissue with their fingers, knuckles and elbows, loosening up the body so it can align with the pull of gravity and work more fluidly. The change that is possible still amazes me.

Rolfers look at the whole body when deciding how best to address a symptom. The ten sessions are based on a "formula" and in addition the Rolfer attends to a client's specific problems.

The formula loosens up the whole body, which automatically provides relief to some of the problem areas and creates new fluidity and increased energy.

My first experience with Rolfing in 1975, while emotionally trying, was physically effective. Even after seven of the ten sessions, my body changed shape and I was able to carry a backpack up trails and hold previously painful Yoga positions. As my head came up and my arms reached forward I looked out to the world with new decisiveness.

In my first Rolfing I was surprised to find that while the Rolfer worked on part of my body I would have a sudden wave of feeling. My upper back, left side, brought on an awareness of my mother and a bristling feeling of wanting to get her away from me. The Rolfer encouraged me to express the feelings to free my tissue of them. Work on my upper thigh produced deep tears of sadness accompanied by a diffuse memory of my brother. When he worked on my mouth and face I became numb and spent an hour in the office before I was able to drive home. At the time I assumed my reactions had to do with many distressing experiences at the dentist. I was not aware that I had been sexually abused and my tissue had recorded information that years later was again provoked into feeling.

Now when Rex or other Rolfers work on me the feelings that come up are milder. I have cleaned most of the painful memories out of my tissues, and only the most deeply buried appear. My pelvis is positioned correctly and my body is in line with the pull of gravity.

People report that after Rolfing sessions on the mouth they find themselves talking more for a time and after sessions on the pelvis they are often angry. Many people make major changes in their lives during or after the sessions. Changes in relationships and jobs are common. People who are in therapy with me become more open to emotional change and more comfortable with their feelings.

When I ask Rolfers why this is so, no one can give a scientific answer. The intuitive answer is that if we significantly alter our physical structure, other parts of life must respond. Our bodies reflect our approach to the world. If our approach changes, we expect to see a physical change. For example, when people feel successful and powerful in their careers they stand taller with head held high. When a Rolfer can change connective tissue so that we stand taller and find our head higher, we can expect to have the corresponding feeling.

If a Rolfer changes the pelvic position that developed in order to protect genitals, then we can expect to awaken the fear such positioning diminished. When these feelings come to the surface they are available to work on. They have become loosened up from the "Thou Shalt Not Be Aware" rule.

If you are curious about Rolfing, you can set up an appointment for the first of the ten session series. At the end of that session you can decide if you want to continue through the series or stop with one. Many Rolfers offer free consultations to help you learn about what they can do for you.

The Rolfer will have you fill out a form with your medical/physical history when you arrive. You will be shown into the Rolfing room and asked to take off everything but your underwear and lie down on the Rolfing table face up. The Rolfer will leave the room while you do this and return when you are ready. A covering sheet is not routinely used, but you can request one. Some Rolfers suggest taking your picture before the first session and after the last to record physical changes in your posture. This is up to you. Most people space their sessions one week apart. Your Rolfer can tell you if it is better to space them further apart.

You can find a Rolfer in your area by looking in the phone book under Rolfing or under massage. If no one is listed (many Rolfers aren't), then write or call:

The Rolf Institute
P.O. Box 1868
Boulder, CO 80306
303-449-5905

They will give you the names of the Rolfers nearest to you.

Trager

Psycho-physical integration, or Trager, is a gentle rocking massage that will help you experience your body and provide a variety of other benefits. It was developed to heal certain body difficulties and carries emotional and psychological gifts as well. During sessions I have had, I experienced the feeling of being an infant cared for by a mother who was tuned in to my needs without any verbal communication. Trager practitioners are trained in the process of "hooking up" with the client, employing their intuitive abilities to perceive what is needed. I get to feel that my needs are being met, even though I cannot articulate what they are, much as a baby can't. While this feeling isn't the intent of the work, the benefit is useful for emotional unfolding.

Having body parts rocked by a person who is very familiar with them and how they work can allow us to experience them more richly. Few of us got enough of this experience.

For information about how to find people in your area, contact:

> The Trager Institute
> Betty Fuller, Director
> 10 Old Mill Street
> Mill Valley, CA 94941
> 415-388-2688

The Feldenkrais Method

The purpose of this form of body work, done with your clothes on, lying on a table, is to bring you awareness of your body. From that awareness, many benefits follow, including increased consciousness of your sexual self. During my first Feldenkrais "lesson," even after much Rolfing and other forms of body work, I could sense blocked awkward places and the free fluid ones in new ways. Judith Marcus, a Seattle practitioner, has gifted hands. I could tell immediately that she was receiving information through her hands and that she was talking to my tissues. For more information about how to find people in your area, contact:

> The Feldenkrais Guild
> P.O. Box 11145
> San Francisco, California 94101

Massage

Massage by a massage therapist who is sensitive to bodies is another useful way to increase our physical awareness. I suggest you obtain referrals from people who have received massage regularly and then check them out. If a massage therapist doesn't seem to really connect with you, or leaves you uncomfortable in

some way, don't go back. As with most professions, there are
very good ones and not so good ones. If you have never had a
good massage, you are missing something quite wonderful.

Movement

A number of movement therapies help unlock body memory
and allow us to join with our bodies to live fully. I present two
here. Increasing body awareness through movement is particularly useful if you are sensitive to touch or are not able to trust
the touch of a body worker. Movement classes are also an inex-
pensive way to learn about your physical container.

Awareness Through Movement (Feldenkrais)

A second Feldenkrais approach to obtaining awareness of
your body is movement instruction. The teacher (in a class or
on audio tape) tells you how to make slow gentle movements
with full attention to what is happening in your body. In contrast to exercise which is an end in itself, these instructions
provide an environment in which you can become aware of the
complexities of your physical nature. Along with awareness
comes the possible release of stored memory.

Yoga

Yoga is one of the world's oldest forms of spiritual exercise,
and it can serve us in our search for improving communication
with our body. I have found the Iyengar method of teaching
Hatha Yoga to be the most useful in relating with parts of my
body. While other methods made me feel good, both limber and
strong, the Iyengar approach fine-tunes Yoga positions in ways
that unavoidably draw my attention to parts of my body. Yoga
teachers can be reached through most holistic health centers or
massage practitioners.

Rolfing Movement Integration

Movement Integration is related to Rolfing, but the focus is
on areas of the body that are not free to move fluidly in relation
to the rest of the body. The practitioner will begin by asking

about what you feel in your body and will watch you move to detect areas that are blocked. She or he will touch your body and ask you to move in certain ways at the same time your body is being moved. New connections are made between muscles and the nervous system. More information can be obtained from the Rolf Institute at the address given earlier.

Alexander Technique

The Alexander Technique is a method of increasing awareness and fluidity of the body through a process of moving to the instructions of the practitioner. The client practices new ways to move, but isn't expected to retain the information consciously or practice it between sessions. The "learning" that is taking place is in the form of neural connections, so you get to see yourself change instead of making yourself change.

Learning From Our Body

As we work to reclaim our physical self, we can use help in our search for what happened physically when we were small. While we look for experiences that are related to our sexuality, we may also find tissue memory of other kinds of mishandling.

Asking Your Body For Information

Begin with some body stretches or movement, including breathing deeply into yourself.

Thinking about the possibility that you were sexually touched when you were too young to remember, and knowing that your body remembers it, what body part comes to mind? (Your "inner voices" may be saying you are making this up, thinking of that body part means nothing and there is no point to continuing. This is a universal reaction when we begin to ask ourselves for information that isn't in conscious memory. For now let yourself "make it up" and postpone the evaluation of accuracy until later.)

Touch and look at that body part. Acknowledge it for its willingness to hold this information for you. Let it know that you will listen.

Give the part a voice. Use your mouth to form words the part wants to say to you or use your pen to write the words.

When it has finished speaking, you may answer.

When the conversation is complete, then stroke or pat the part and thank it for sharing the information with you.

It's okay not to believe what you just said. Developing a relationship with your body parts takes time.

15

Allowing Our Creativity

We all want to tell our stories, and in fact we all do. Our stories get told through our sexual behavior, our choice of partners, expressions we carry on our faces and positioning of our bodies. Because the need to tell is counteracted by the powerful rule "Thou Shalt Not Be Aware," our story does not get to be in our conscious mind; but it remains within, waiting to be heard. Becoming a good therapist includes learning to read stories that can't yet be spoken and presenting a mirror to the client for the story that is searching for an audience.

One reason we are creative is to tell the repressed story so we can free ourselves of its effects (See Alice Miller's, *The Untouched Key*). You can use this function as you bring your story to consciousness. If you have a well-developed creative medium, you can examine your creations for information. If you don't already have a medium, one may come up that you can allow to unfold. If you have always wanted to take an art or pottery class or voice lessons or creative writing, now is the time. If you do the art for the art alone, *with no intention of telling your story*, you are more likely to tell it. *After* the work is done go back and examine it as if it were done by someone else.

I want to tell you stories of two people who recognize how they have used art to enhance their sexual unfolding. The first story is mine. The second is Rex's.

My Story

Writing is my creative arena. Two years ago I thought I had completed my sexual healing because I was having wonderful sex with Rex and no more major issues were coming up. Then when I was on a plane from Anchorage to Seattle, exhausted from three long days of work, a book formed itself in my head and demanded to be written down. I sat up and spent the three-hour trip working on the outline. It was clear to me that I could not prevent this project — it would have to be done.

As I wrote in any spare moment I could find, I learned a great deal. The numbers of books I read mounted but felt effortless, as if I hadn't read anything. I absorbed everything going on around me that had to do with sexual energy. It was effortless because my creativity pulled me where I had to go. My task was altering my life so I could respect the process and allow it to unfold. I felt as compulsive about it as I had with addictive behaviors in the past.

As I moved along in the process of finding an agent and a publisher, I confronted major fears that immobilized me for weeks. I was now communicating things that thus far had been between me, my computer and a few chosen friends, doing so in a way that could be *seen by anyone*. But I couldn't turn back — when creativity has its grip on me, I must follow.

The next step was giving a public lecture on the subject of healthy sexual energy. I set it up, and in spite of my prior experience talking and teaching I knew this would be difficult. I was talking about *my* ideas about incest, triangulation and sex. I spent many hours preparing, almost memorizing the talk and creating nine pages of notes. I had acupuncture needles to reduce fear and I did hours of emotional work — to no avail. Frozen into a numb state, I got up in front of 50 people and recited my speech.

As I drove home that night, filled with shame, I found it hard to trust that my creativity would lead me in the right direction. But the next morning I woke up clear. Giving this particular talk had ensured that I would finally communicate two of my issues. First, my subject was sex, the unmentionable that was kept secret as I grew up. Now it was no longer secret. And second, the dysfunctional family requirement that I not speak the truth was deeply imbedded in me. My patterns said if I spoke the truth about the incest that was emerging in my memories I would be shot in front of a firing squad.

The next step became obvious. I called my mother and arranged to meet with her the next day. I knew I had to tell her that my father had sexually abused me when I was very young and I had not been able to talk about it. This conversation opened doors to further talks about what really went on. I broke the rule, I wasn't killed and — totally unexpectedly — I was heard by my mother.

Once the rule was broken and I could be aware, memories came back quickly. The foggy ones cleared up. This increased awareness allowed me to see many more dysfunctional family issues that I had denied. Things that had been fuzzy questions became obvious realities.

My creativity was getting me to talk and chose a medium that forced me to talk. As I look back on the time when I began the book, the true task was already apparent although I wasn't able to see it until much later. I began seriously writing when on vacation. I had been looking forward to expanding the outline and seeing what would unfold, and that was my first chance. But I couldn't write. I soon sensed that I had to tell my mother what I was doing because she was the one my voices said would kill me if she found out. So I sent off a letter telling her explicitly about the book. As I put the letter in the mail slot, I knew I could begin writing. My fate was already determined so I had nothing to lose.

Rex's Story

Rex is a survivor of incest and has used pottery to bring forth many buried memories. The creative process began after he had retrieved several memories of his father interacting sexually with him when he was under three.

Rex has a background in art, particularly with clay, but he hadn't done much for a time besides sculpting bodies with Rolfing. Signing up for a pottery class set a process in motion. Immediately he began to view me as his mother. He was sure I didn't want him going to the pottery studio and would want a report of everything that happened when he got home. He would say he would be home at 5:00 when he really wanted to stay until 7:00, and then he would come home at 6:00 to face my anger.

As we worked these things through, he became aware he had feelings about his mother that our relationship allowed him to express. His father's shame had been communicated to him non-verbally along with the prohibition against letting his mother know anything sexual was going on between them. She had become the unconscious enemy of Rex's need to tell his story. As he projected her role onto me I became the enemy of the expression of incest through pottery — even though Rex had no conscious idea he was telling his incest story.

He went to the studio a lot, turning out many pieces. His fingers move slowly and yet forms emerge from the clay quickly. Some of his pieces brought up strong feelings for me when I first saw them, but I was not aware that emotional work was occurring. Then he walked into my office holding a brown pot with white glaze between the two segments, and my mouth fell open. I said, "That's testicles with semen running between them!" The look on his face confirmed that I was right. His creativity had bypassed his conscious mind and traveled through his fingers onto the clay. He was telling his story without knowing he was telling it.

More pieces showed up, some that we could now recognize as relatives to the ones we understood. A group appeared that seemed significant and evoked emotion in many of our clients who had the opportunity to look at them in the waiting room. These pots are mounds of clay in different shapes with one mouth on each. The mouths have expressions that evoked people's emotions ranging from distaste to fear to sadness. We assumed it was a child's mouth that wanted to speak. He even named some of the pots based on this belief.

One morning we were talking about men who use babies for sexual gratification. Rex was describing how a baby must look to a man who has entered an addictive sexual trance, is focused on having an orgasm and sees the baby's fleshy body as available. Young babies suck reflexively — even on penises. As I listened to him it dawned on me: Those pots were babies, and the mouths were used to put penises in. The rest of the body was indistinct because the person in a trance wouldn't be aware of the baby, only the mouth and the flesh. As I told Rex, his face again confirmed what I had seen, and we rushed to look at one of the pots.

Rex's fingers had given form to his role in his father's eyes. He communicated to the world that he had been sexually violated, and how.

As I write this, Rex is experiencing fear that inhibits his creativity because his images have become conscious. He made a huge penis and testicles that are the size they would look to a baby. He wants to do a show with the story of his incest and recovery. But now that he knows what he is doing, he doesn't have the anonymity of repression.

Many years ago Rex did a series of "erotic art" drawings. Because he had a name for his style he never questioned why he chose the subjects he did. They merely appeared out of his pencils in the same way his pots showed up.

I had not seen these pictures because they are owned by a friend of Rex's in another city, so he was describing them to me in detail some months after he began retrieving memories of his father's incestuous activities. The pictures he described perfectly fit the memories that were now able to take conscious form. This time both our faces lit up at the same time as we saw the connections.

16

Onward:
A Look Into
The Future

We are working on reclaiming our innocent, healthy sexual energy. As we evolve, more and more of us won't respond to the seductions of our culture. We can learn to be aware of ways our sexual energy has been distorted, to see the lure of our culture's beliefs and to become aware that we cannot have our spiritual sexuality as long as we unquestioningly obey our culture.

As sex-laced advertising becomes ineffective it will diminish in use. When men no longer respond sexually to women dressed and moving to attract their sexual attention, women will stop presenting themselves as sex objects. When women no longer associate their worth with "sexual" attractiveness, they will stop dressing and acting in ways to get men to feel sexual. And men will get a chance to see the whole woman.

As we open our eyes to our sexuality, we are opening ourselves to a process that encompasses *everything*. Sexuality is only one component of our spiritual nature. As we open to purifying one aspect of ourselves, then we open to all the rest as well. As one area of addictiveness heals it is natural to move on to the next and the next.

Those of us with intuitive vision know we cannot live within the culture as it is. We also know we don't have good models for the culture that is coming. Our culture evolves as we evolve, so the models we find are only a little farther along. We will all create the new culture together.

I define "culture" as predictable ways most of us behave that have been passed down through the generations, tempered by more recent changes brought about by the contagious influence of visionaries. The sexual revolution was an attempt to change our culture's repression of sexuality. It resulted in powerful opening up of the sexual arena, allowing people to have more choice about their activities. This change mingled with the remaining cultural dictates, such as the belief in a sex drive and the sexual response to body parts, and produced some negative effects such as socially accepted casual sex. Sex addiction flourished, actually encouraged by the cultural changes. We are moving now into the next phase of enlightened sexuality, which includes examining our right to not be sexual and to be monogamous because it feels right. "Casual sex" will no longer exist because all sex, even if only experienced once between a couple, won't be "casual."

As you relinquish your cross-wiring, you won't fit in any longer. People who flirt at parties will be uncomfortable when you don't, much as drinkers are not comfortable with those who don't drink. You will be excluded by groups of people who bond with flirtatious sexual energy because you will be a reminder of what they are doing. You will be criticized for not being romantic. You will frighten those who believe their self-worth is tied to your sexual interest. People often cover fear with anger, so you will also have people angry with you and trying to get you to change. Your family of origin will be upset by you. You won't belong.

You will belong instead to a new order of people, those who are recovering from addictiveness. You will be mirrored by those in your supportive network and you will be a mirror for others. Over time you will see increasing numbers of those like yourself increase and decreasing numbers of those who object. As the objectors decrease, it will be more and more surprising when you see them pop up occasionally. You will tell your story with awe and amazement. Eventually you may find your healthy sexual energy is such a part of you that your conscious mind won't be bothered by thoughts of it. It is yours. And then another layer of addictiveness will show up for you to work on.

APPENDIX I: FEELINGS

I. Up, Positive

happy and positive
awake
basking
bright
celebrating
colorful
confident
confirmed
delight
delighted
eager
enlightened
enriched
equal
fascinated
filled up
firm
funny
gentle
harmonious
hopeful
jovial
joyful
new
on
open
pleased
proud
radiant
rambunctious
ready
real
refreshed
relieved
renewed
resilient
rhythmic
rooted
safe
sensational
serene
smart
solid
spontaneous
supported
tickled
vibrant
witty
wondrous

loved
adorable
adored
appreciated
bolstered
embraced
cherished
wanted
warm and fuzzy
supported
heard
listened to
seen
valued

loving
friendly
self-loving
warm
affectionate
endearing
smiling
giving
wanting

passionate
challenged
consumed
enlivened
high
powerful
firm
hearty
whole
connected
going for it
out there

peaceful
blissful
comfortable
integrated
soft
tranquil
trusting
calm
serene
loving

articulate
contemplative
intellectual
introspective
rational
clear

creative
curious
inventive
compelled
expressive
wondering
interested
spontaneous
delighted

excited
exhilarated
hyper
energized
anticipating
manic
ready to go
aroused

II. Body Feelings

body feelings
achy
active
alive
lively
bloated
cat-like
contaminated
clumsy
dirty
energetic

213

.exhausted
fat
fluid
full
gluttonous
groggy
healthy
in pain
lazy
listless
loose
nauseated
physical
ravenous
rested
sick
skinny
slow
sluggish
squishy
starving
tension
tense
tight
tired
succulent
unclean
uncoordinated
vain
vigorous
voluptuous
warm
weary
wired

sexual
aroused
lusting
desirous
plump
open
fearful
worried
loving
delighted

ashamed
compulsive
hidden
passionate
unloved
body feelings
full

III. Down

depressed
absent
alienated
bored
chilled
closed
contained
dead
disintegrated
down
drugged
dull
empty
frozen
gone
hopeless
inferior
low
not belonging
nothing
numb
off
remote
removed
suppressed
tearful
tenuous
withdrawn
slow motion

afraid
apprehensive
cautious
desperate
dread
exposed

fearful
frightened
cold
horrified
leery
nervous
serious
shocked
terrified
vulnerable
wary
watchful
worried

ashamed
embarrassed
false
filthy
guilty
humiliated
remorseful
dirty
sinful
shameful
wrong
degraded
little
scolded
belittled

abandoned
lonely
longing
dying
unfair
left
rejected
overlooked
betrayed
dispensable
vengeful
stoic
desperate

dumb
retarded
silly

stupid
ashamed
down
failure

sad
tearful
grieving
down
unloved
empty
alone
yearning
pained

inferior
apologetic
submissive
subordinate
victimized
one-down
worthless
hopeless

IV. Down, Negative

angry
abrupt
abusive
annoyed
brutal
caustic
dictatorial
disgusted
enraged
explosive
frustrated
furious
haughty
hostile
jeering
mischievous
moody
pissed
provoked
resentful
sarcastic

spiteful
suspicious
tyrannical
vindictive
volatile

*anxious and
defensive*
agitated
bristly
cunning
defensive
fragile
frantic
hidden
polite
proper
rebellious
repressed
resistive
scared
scrappy
shaky
stubborn
tense
terse
tight
worried
terrified
hostile

driven
compulsive
obligated
obsessed
talkative
tenacious
demanding
out of control
blind
desperate
empty
wired

yearning
itchy
wanting

hopeful
hungry
empty
bitter
hopeless
angry
grieving
waiting
restless
irritable

V. Abused

abused
attacked
belittled
contaminated
criticized
crushed
diminished
disappointed
discounted
harassed
heckled
helpless
hurt
minimized
negated
pawn-like
put down
rejected
restrained
sucked on
teased
tired
tortured
victimized

VI. Awkward Or Confused

awkward
awful
unreal
worthless
dispensable

dorky
clumsy
difficult
ungrounded
off
body feelings
off balance
self conscious

confused
ambivalent
in conflict
irrational
jostled
mercurial
misfit
puzzled
quizzical
tempted
tumultuous
wondering
shaken
dazed

unsettled
chaotic
crazy
ruffled
rushed
self conscious
shifty
stressed out

VII. Other

revulsion
sour
superior
disgust
rage
nauseated
negative

anticipating
expectant
searching
waiting

wondering
excited
eager
body feelings
dread
yearning
afraid

APPENDIX II:
VISUALIZATIONS

Instructions For All Visualizations

Preparing Your Environment

Make yourself comfortable, preferably lying down on the floor. (Beds aren't good because of their association with sleep.) Remove anything that distracts you from images elicited by the visualization. Check the room temperature, intruding noises, body positioning and anything else that draws your attention away from yourself.

Reading The Visualization

You can read the instructions into a tape recorder, and use the tape with a group or by yourself. It is also possible to read to one other person and take turns.

Long pauses are indicated by the dots. The shorter series of dots indicates about five seconds and the longer ones 10 to 15 seconds. Before you read the instructions, allow yourself to enter a calm, relaxed state and allow your voice to flow out softly. You want your listeners to attend to the words you say, rather than you or your speaking style.

Relaxation

Following is one way to relax your body before beginning the visualization.

Take three or more deep breaths. On the first breath notice how far into your body the air flows. We are capable of filling ourselves from pubic bone to shoulders, but most of us have many restrictions in our bodies that prevent full expansion of our lungs and surrounding tissue.

On the second breath, pay attention to your entire torso and see how much air you are pulling in.

Continuing to breathe deeply, check your body for places you hold tension and breathe air into them. Begin with your toes, your feet and ankles. Breathe life into them, and breathe tension out . . . .

Checking your calves, . . . knees . . . . and then thighs . . . . Breathe life in and flush tension out . . . . Now your abdomen . . . . and chest . . . . Breathe life in and flush tension out . . . . Buttocks and lower back . . . . Upper back . . . . Breathe . . . . Shoulders, . . . their fronts, . . . their backs . . . their sides . . . . Breathe . . . . Upper arms, . . . elbows, . . . lower arms, . . . hands, . . . fingers . . . . Now focus on your neck . . . notice how it fits into your torso. Let it sink in to you, then rise up out of you . . . . . Breathe . . . . Your face holds expression all day — let it rest now . . . and take any form it wants. Perhaps your mouth will fall open. Let the roof of your mouth relax, ... your jaw submit to gravity . . . . . . And breathe.

Relax for another minute before we go on.

I. You Were Shamed

Think for a moment about shame. . . . You were shamed for being in a human body, for being a sexual person. These feelings of shame are carried in your body, now, and they don't belong there. Your sexual feelings were good and pure, nothing to be ashamed of. Now you can clean these feelings out of you. What brings up feelings of shame when you think of sex? Of your sexuality? What are you "ashamed of?" Let the feeling of shame emerge in your body. Take a minute to be with this painful feeling. (Allow about 30 seconds.) Where do you feel shame in your body? (Allow another 30 seconds.) What's the shame doing now? (Allow about 20 seconds.)

Now let these thoughts and feelings go from your awareness. Let them fall back into the recesses of your mind.

When you are ready, allow yourself to move gently up and out of your body, drifting slowly back over time. Look down on each of the passing times of your life . . . . . first the adult years . . . . then the young adult times . . . . and back to the teen years, high school, junior high . . . then back through puberty on to grade school . . . . scan each era for the places, the people and the times that stand out . . . . Now visit the time before you were in school . . . . . . back to when you stood by the table and just barely saw over the top . . . . and then back to diapers and walking wasn't very certain . . . . then to when you were just a small baby, carried everywhere . . . .

Let your mind roam over all these times and settle on one that stands out to you. It can be from any age . . . . when you have selected a time, allow a scene to appear. It can seem invented or real. Look around you. What do you see? . . . . What do you hear? . . . . Who is there? . . . . What are you feeling? . . . . Look down at your little body. How does it look to you? . . . . Has anyone shamed your body? . . . . Who can you bring into this scene who can look at your body with clean appreciation? . . . . If you choose, bring them here now . . . . What does this person do? And say? . . . . What happened? . . . . What are you feeling? . . . . Is there something you want to do in this scene? . . . . You can take time now to do it if you wish . . . . What happened? . . . . What are you feeling? . . . . Is there anyone you need to speak to? . . . . What do you want to say? . . . . When you are ready to leave this scene, notice what you need to do to say goodbye . . . . then do it . . . . When you are ready, make the transition back through the years going forward this time, until you float in this time . . . . Before returning to your body, hover at the ceiling and look down at the people in the room . . . . What do you see? . . . . What do you feel? . . . . Now gently slide back into your body . . . . and when you are ready, open your eyes.

II. How Are You "Telling Your Story?"

Relax your body with the relaxation instructions given previously. Breathe.

Remember for a moment that we all tell our stories from childhood through our actions, body positioning, faces, body memories and feelings towards others. Pay attention to your body. Remember those feelings that appear, seemingly out of the blue. Remember that many times during your childhood you were told you were wrong. You were told not to feel. You were shamed for just being you.

After a few minutes, allow these thoughts and awarenesses to drop from mind and focus instead on the task of the imagery.

When you are ready, allow yourself to move gently up and out of your body, drifting slowly back over time. Look down on each of the passing times of your life . . . . . first the adult years . . . . then the young adult times . . . . . . and back to the teen years, high school, junior high . . . . then back through puberty on to grade school . . . . scan each era for the places, the people and the times that stand out . . . . Now visit the time before you were in school . . . . back to when you stood by the table and just barely saw over the top . . . . and then back to diapers and walking wasn't very certain . . . . . . then to when you were just a small baby, carried everywhere . . . .

Let your mind roam over all these times and settle on one that stands out to you. It can be from any age . . . . when you have selected a time, allow a scene to appear. It can seem invented or real. Look around you. What do you see? . . . . What do you hear? . . . . Who is there? . . . . What are you feeling? . . . . What feelings are you supposed to hold back? . . . . What will happen if you don't hold them back? . . . . If you could, what would you tell? . . . . Who would listen with respect and belief? . . . .

Imagine that your adult self enters the scene now. The adult you who knows exactly what you need. Now what happens? . . . . What are you feeling? . . . . What do you want to do? . . . . You can do it now . . . . What happened? . . . . What are you feeling? . . . . Is there anyone you need to speak to? . . . . What do you want to say? . . . . When you are ready to leave this scene, notice what you need to do to say goodbye . . . . and then do it . . . . when you are ready, make the transition back through the years going forward this time, until you float in the present . . . . Before returning to your body, hover at the ceiling and look down at the people in the room . . . . What do you see? . . . . What do you feel? . . . . Now gently, slide back into your body . . . . and when you are ready, open your eyes.

III. Protecting Your "Child"

Relax your body with the relaxation instructions given previously. Breathe.

Remember for a moment that deep within you is a part of you that *knows*. That knows everything. Your "inner child." The part of you that lived through your childhood, who knew you depended on the grown-ups to keep you alive, who knew what was best for you and knew when the best wasn't happening. That little child still remembers being born with curiosity about life, being curious and ready to live fully, wanting to do everything with everyone. And that little child who remembers all the hurts, being told not to feel and being told to be different than you are. The little child who was shamed for just being you, for being curious about sexual stuff, shamed for wanting to touch and explore. That little person is still inside of you, still knowing everything. And this child is telling your story by getting you to act in certain ways, showing with your body, with your expressions. This child is trying to be heard by you as well as by others. The little child wants you to listen. It is possible to let that little child speak to you to let you know what happened, and to let you know what is needed now, and how to take care of this young person. How to raise that little child yourself . . . .

So now let these thoughts drop from your mind, let your mind go blank and we'll move on to the imagery.

Now allow yourself to move gently up and out of your body . . . . drifting slowly back over time. Look down on each of the passing times of your life . . . . . . starting with the adult years . . . . and moving back to the young adult times . . . high school, and junior high . . . . Let the people and the times and the places stand out . . . . then moving back through puberty to the time before you became a young adult to grade school . . . . Then visit the time before you were in school . . . . preschool . . . . then even younger than that, when you stood by the table and just barely saw over the top . . . . even if memories don't come, you can imagine what that was like for you . . . . . and then back to when you were just learning how to walk, you were pretty little . . . . then to when you were just a tiny baby, being carried everywhere you went and having your needs met by other people . . . .

So let your mind roam over all these times we have just revisited, and settle on one that stands out to you. It can be from any age . . . . and when you have selected a time, allow a scene to appear. It can seem made up or real. When you are in that scene, look around you. What do you see? . . . . And what do you hear? . . . . And who else is there with you? . . . . What are you feeling? . . . . Are there feelings that you are supposed to hold back? .

. . . . What will happen if you don't hold them back? . . . . If you had someone who could listen and would, what would you tell? . . . . What happens if you tell them? . . . . Did you make a decision about how you would be when you were little? If so, what was it? . . . . Do you know how this decision helps you? . . . . If you made a decision when you were little, honor yourself for making a decision that would make life go more easily . . . . Then you might take a look at how that decision interfered later in your life . . . .

Now imagine that your adult self enters the scene. The adult you who knows exactly what you need and who can protect you, who really sees you. And now what happens? . . . . What are you feeling? . . . .

Is there something more you want to do in this scene? . . . . You can go ahead and do it now . . . . If possible, tell your adult self what the story is that needs to be told . . . . What are you feeling? . . . . How does your adult self respond? . . . . Now in preparation for leaving this scene, what do you need to do to say goodbye? And go ahead and do it . . . . when you finish saying goodbye, then move slowly back across the years, growing up . . . . And when you're back to this time, slide gently into your body . . . . and when you are ready, open your eyes.

IV. What Are Your Sexual Fantasies?

Relax your body with the relaxation instructions given previously. Breathe.

Remember for a moment that all people have sexual fantasies — it is in part because we live in a culture that keeps us alienated from each other, so we fantasize closeness. It is also because our sexual feelings were cross-wired with many things they don't belong with, and our fantasies are telling the story. Sexual fantasies are not something to feel shame about — they just *are*. And they hold information for you about cross-wired sexual feelings and the things your childhood and our culture imposed on you. Things that can now be released. Keep breathing.

Sexual fantasies are those thoughts that come up when you are having sex that are about someone else or you are doing something else or you are somewhere else. They are thoughts that come up when you see a sexually attractive person and imagine being sexual with her or him. They are sexual thoughts about your lover or potential lover. They are also sexual thoughts that come up when you are feeling low and want to feel better. They are images you use when you masturbate that will arouse you and distract you from the present. Sexual fantasies include those romantic dreams of finding the right man or woman or falling passionately in love. Keep breathing.

Allow your mind now to scan over the fantasies that you have . . . . Select one . . . . Let it play out in your mind . . . . let it play very slowly . . . . As it does, pay attention to what you are feeling . . . . Notice the details . . . . If sexual arousal comes up, just let it come. Just notice it . . . . If shame comes up, breathe through it and let it flow . . . . When you are finished with the fantasy, ask yourself what may have happened in childhood that your fantasy is trying to tell you about now. This question may not have an answer. That's fine. Just pay attention to what happens when you ask the question . . . . When you are ready, return to the present and open your eyes.

V. What Are Your Early Sexual Memories?

Relax your body with the relaxation instructions given previously. Breathe.

Think for a moment about your sexual self. Remember that you are sexual, and you have been from before you were born. As far back as you can remember, you had sexual feelings. Sometimes they were in your genitals, but other times you felt them in your mouth or your anus or on your skin. When you were born, you liked being a sexual person, but as you spent more time in the world, things were done to your sexuality that made it seem not so pure and delightful. It is possible to remove the shame now so that you can have that delight in your sexual self again. You *can* remember and let the feelings of shame wash out and free your body of the poisons.

First, we'll find some sexual memories, one at a time, that you can choose from. So let a sexual memory come into your mind. Any memory from any time . . . . Let your mind wander over it. What do you feel? Let all the feelings come so they can tell you more than you know now. When you have looked this memory over, put it on a shelf so you can return to it later if you wish. Now let an earlier memory come up. It doesn't have to be from childhood . . . . examine this one, too, and have your feelings . . . . Then put it on the shelf, waiting for later . . . . Now ask yourself, what is the earliest sexual memory that will come into your mind . . . . Take what time you need . . . . Let the feelings come with it . . . . Now put *it* on the shelf with the other two. Look them over, and decide which one you want to look at further . . . . Take it off the shelf and open it up. Let this memory play out in detail. How does it begin? . . . . Is anyone there with you? . . . . Notice your feelings . . . . . . Let them flow . . . . Then what happens? . . . . Make up what happens next . . . . And then what happens next? . . . . Now you can tell this memory the way you *want* it to happen. You might bring in an ally or your adult self. You could make yourself grown-up all of a sudden. However you want this memory to go next, you can make it happen. What happens? . . . . Notice your feelings. Let them flow . . . . .Remember that your body is a wonderful, sexual container . . . . When you are ready, return to the present and open your eyes.

SUGGESTED READING

I. Books About Sexual Recovery

Allen, Charlotte Vale, **Daddy's Girl,** Berkley Publications, 1984.

Carnes, Patrick, **Contrary to Love, Helping the Sexual Addict,** CompCare, 1989.

Carnes, Patrick, **Out of the Shadows: Understanding Sexual Addiction,** CompCare, 1983.

Earle, Ralph and Gregory Crow, **Lonely all the Time,** Pocket Books, 1989.

Engel, Beverly, **The Right to Innocence,** Jeremy Tarcher, 1989.

Fraser, Sylvia, **My Father's House,** Harper & Row, 1987.

Hunter, Mic, **Abused Boys, the Neglected Victims of Sexual Abuse,** Lexington, 1990.

Kasl, Charlotte, **Women, Sex and Addiction,** Ticknor and Fields, 1989.

Love, Patricia, **The Emotional Incest Syndrome,** Bantam, 1990.

Miller, Alice, **Thou Shalt Not Be Aware: Society's Betrayal Of The Child,** Meridian, 1986.

Schaef, Anne Wilson, **Escape From Intimacy,** Harper & Row, 1989.

Wisechild, Louise, **The Obsidian Mirror,** Seal Press, 1988.

II. Books About General Recovery

Beatty, Melody, **Co-dependent No More: How to Stop Controlling Others and Love Yourself More,** Harper/Hazelden, 1987.

Bradshaw, John, **Healing the Shame that Binds You,** Health Communications, 1988.

Farmer, Steven, **Adult Children of Abusive Parents,** Contemporary Books, 1989.

Goldberg, Herb, **The Hazards of Being Male: Surviving the Myths of Masculine Privilege,** Signet, 1977.

Goldberg, Herb, **The Inner Male: Overcoming Roadblocks to Intimacy,** Signet, 1988.

Goldberg, Herb, **The New Male Female Relationship,** Signet, 1983.

Goldberg, Herb, **The New Male: From Self-Destruction to Self-Care,** Signet, 1980.

Lee, John, **I Don't Want to be Alone,** Health Communications, 1990.

Miller, Alice, **Banished Knowledge: Facing Childhood Injuries,** Doubleday, 1990.

Miller, Alice, **For Your Own Good: Hidden Cruelty in Child-Rearing and the Roots of Violence,** Farrar, Strauss, Giroux, 1984.

Miller, Alice, **The Untouched Key,** Doubleday, 1990.

Schaef, Anne Wilson, **Co-dependence: Misunderstood, Mistreated,** Harper & Row, 1986.

Schaef, Anne Wilson, **When Society Becomes an Addict,** Harper & Row, 1989.

P. 96 - Harville Henderson —
   Getting the Love You Want

Henderson — Harville p. 408